TRUE

and FALSE

REPENTANCE

THE CHARLES G. FINNEY
MEMORIAL LIBRARY

Evangelistic Sermon Series
- So Great Salvation
- The Guilt of Sin
- True and False Repentance
- God's Love for a Sinning World

Revival Sermon Series
- Victory Over the World
- True Saints
- True Submission

Sermons on Prayer
- Prevailing Prayer

TRUE
and
FALSE
REPENTANCE

Evangelistic Messages

CHARLES G. FINNEY

KREGEL PUBLICATIONS
GRAND RAPIDS, MICHIGAN 49501

True and False Repentance, by Charles G. Finney.
© 1966 by Kregel Publications, a division of
Kregel, Inc., P. O. Box 2607, Grand Rapids, MI
49501. All rights reserved. This series of sermons
selected from *Lectures to Professing Christians* and
Gospel Themes by Charles G. Finney.

Library of Congress Catalog Card No. 66-10576

ISBN 0-8254-2617-0

7 8 9 10 Printing / Year 94 93 92 91

Printed in the United States of America

PUBLISHER'S FOREWORD

Why this new edition of the sermons of Charles Grandison Finney? Because in many ways the days in which we are living are a duplicate of the day and situation in which Finney himself proclaimed the message which God had given him — the call to evangelism and to revival. These messages speak to our day in no uncertain sound for conditions within the church, and in the world around, call for a voice from God, a resounding clarion call for return to the Biblical standard of Christian life, and the God-ordained plan of redemption and revival.

These have been chosen and arranged with the needs of the world and church today in view. They are as applicable in this day of falling away and departure from the faith as they were in Finney's day. Heart-searching and uncompromising, they cut away the froth and frills so apparent in much modern preaching to reveal God's message for a sinning world, a world seemingly intent upon self-destruction and self-aggrandizement.

It is the publisher's prayer that these messages in their new form will convey God's message to our needy world, revealing His will and purpose for His Church — and His divine plan of salvation for an unbelieving generation.

The Publishers

CONTENTS

1

TRUE AND FALSE REPENTANCE

For godly sorrow worketh repentance to salvation, not to be repented of; but the sorrow of the world worketh death.—2 Cor. vii. 10

IN this chapter the apostle refers to another epistle which he had formerly written to the church at Corinth, on a certain subject, in which they were greatly to blame. He speaks here of the effect that it had, in bringing them to true repentance. They sorrowed after a godly sort. This was the evidence that their repentance was genuine.

"For behold this self-same thing, that ye sorrowed after a godly sort, what carefulness it wrought in you, yea, what clearing of yourselves, yea, what indignation, yea, what fear, yea, what vehement desire, yea, what zeal, yea, what revenge! In all things ye have approved yourselves to be clear in this matter."

In the verse which I have taken for my text, he speaks of two kinds of sorrow for sin, one working repentance unto salvation, the other working death. He alludes to what is generally understood by two kinds of repentance. And this is the subject of discourse to-night.

TRUE AND FALSE REPENTANCE

In discoursing on the subject, I design to show,

I. What true repentance is.

II. How it may be known.

III. What is false and spurious repentance.

IV. How it may be known.

It is high time professors of religion were taught to discriminate much more than they do in regard to the nature and character of various exercises on the subject of religion. Were it so the church would not be so overrun with false and unprofitable professors. I have, of late, been frequently led to examine, over and over again, the reason why there is so much spurious religion, and I have sought to know what is the foundation of the difficulty. That multitudes suppose themselves to be religious, who are not so, unless the Bible is false, is notorious. Why is it that so many are deceived? Why do so many, who are yet impenitent sinners, get the idea that they have repented? The cause is doubtless a want of discriminating instruction respecting the foundation of religion, and especially a want of discrimination respecting true and false repentance.

I. I am to show what is true repentance.

It involves a change of opinion respecting the nature of sin, and this change of opinion followed by a corresponding change of feeling towards sin. Feeling is the result of thought. And when this change of opinion is such as to produce a corresponding change of feeling, if the opinion is right and the feeling corresponds, this is true repentance. It must be right opinion. The opinion now adopted might be such an opinion as God holds respecting sin. Godly sorrow, such as God requires, must spring from such views of sin as God holds.

First. There must be a change of opinion in regard to sin.

1. A change of opinion in regard to the nature of sin.

To one who truly repents sin looks like a very different thing from what it does to him who has not repented. Instead of looking like a thing that is desirable or fascinating, it looks the very opposite, most odious and detestable, and he is astonished at himself, that he ever could have desired such a thing. Impenitent sinners may look at sin and see that it will ruin them, because God will punish them for it; but, after all, it appears in itself desirable; they love it; they roll it under their tongue. If it could end in happiness, they never would think of abandoning it. But to the other it is different; he looks at his own conduct as perfectly hateful. He looks back upon it, and exclaims, "How hateful, how detestable, how worthy of hell, such and such a thing was in me."

2. A change of opinion of the character of sin as respects its relation to God.

Sinners do not see why God threatens sin with such terrible punishment. They love it so well themselves, that they cannot see why God should look at it in such a light as to think it worthy of everlasting punishment. When they are strongly convicted, they see it differently, and so far as opinion is concerned, they see it in the same light that a Christian does, and then they only want a corresponding change of feeling to become Christians. Many a sinner sees its relation to God to be such that it deserves eternal death, but his heart does not go with his opinions. This is the case with the devils and wicked spirits in hell. Mark, then!—a change of opinion is indispensable to true repentance, and always precedes it. The heart never goes out to God in true repentance without a previous change of opinion. There may be a change of opinion without repentance, but no genuine repentance without a change of opinion.

3. A change of opinion in regard to the tendencies of sin.

Before the sinner thinks it utterly incredible that sin should have such tendencies as to deserve everlasting death. He may be fully changed, however, as to his opinions on this point without repentance, but it is impossible a man should truly repent without a change of opinion. He sees sin, in its tendency, as ruinous to himself and everybody else, soul and body, for time and eternity, and at variance with all that is lovely and happy in the universe. He sees that sin is calculated in its tendencies to injure himself and everybody else, and that there is no remedy but universal abstinence. The devil knows it to be so. And possibly there are some sinners now in this congregation who know it.

4. A change of opinion in regard to the desert of sin.

The word rendered repentance implies all this. It implies a change in the state of the mind including all this. The careless sinner is almost devoid of right ideas, even so far as this life is concerned, respecting the desert of sin. Suppose he admits in theory that sin deserves eternal death, he does not believe it. If he believed it, it would be impossible for him to remain a careless sinner. He is deceived, if he supposes that he honestly holds such an opinion as that sin deserves the wrath of God for ever. But the truly awakened and convicted sinner has no more doubt of this than he has of the existence of God. He sees clearly that sin must deserve everlasting punishment from God. He knows that this is a simple matter of fact.

Secondly. In true repentance there must be a corresponding change of feeling.

The change of feeling respects sin in all these particulars, its nature, its relations, its tendencies, and its deserts. The individual who truly repents, not only sees sin to be detestable and vile, and worthy of abhorrence, but he really abhors it, and hates it in his heart. A person may see sin to be hurtful and abominable, while yet his heart loves it, and desires it, and clings to it. But when he truly repents, he most heartily abhors and renounces it.

In relation to God, he feels towards sin as it really is. And here is the source of those gushings of sorrow in which Christians sometimes break out, when contemplating sin. The Christian views it as to its nature, and simply feels abhorrence. But when he views it in relation to God, then he weeps; the fountains of his sorrow gush forth, and he wants to get right down on his face and pour out a flood of tears over his sins.

Then as to the tendencies of sin, the individual who truly repents feels it as it is. When he views sin in its tendencies, it awakens a vehement desire to stop it, and to save people from their sins, and roll back the tide of death. It sets his heart on fire, and he goes to praying, and laboring, and pulling sinners out of the fire with all his might, to save them from the awful tendencies of sin. When the Christian sets his mind on this, he will bestir himself to make people give up their sins. Just as if he saw all the people taking poison which he knew would destroy them, and he lifts up his voice to warn them to *beware*.

He feels right, as to the desert of sin. He has not only an intellectual conviction that sin deserves everlasting punishment, but he feels that it would be so right and so reasonable, and so just, for God to condemn him to eternal death, that so far from finding fault with the sentence of the law that condemns him, he thinks it the wonder of heaven, a wonder of wonders, if God can forgive him. Instead of thinking it hard, or severe, or unkind in God, that incorrigible sinners are sent to hell, he is full of adoring wonder that he is not sent to hell himself, and that this whole guilty world has not long since been hurled down to endless burnings. It is the last thing in the world he would think to complain of, that all sinners are not saved; but O, it is a wonder of mercy that all the world is not damned. And when he thinks of such a sinner's being saved, he feels a sense of gratitude that he never knew anything of till he was a Christian.

II. I am to show what are the works or effects of genuine repentance.

I wish to show you what are the works of true repentance, and to make it so plain to your minds, that you can know infallibly whether you have repented or not.

1. If your repentance is genuine, there is in your mind a conscious change of views and feeling in regard to sin.

Of this you will be just as conscious as you ever were of a change of views and feelings on any other subject. Now, can you say this? Do *you* know, that on this point there has been a change in you, and that old things are done away and all things have become new.

2. Where repentance is genuine, the disposition to repeat sin is gone.

If you have truly repented, you do not now love sin; you do not now abstain from it through fear, and to avoid punishment, but because you hate it. How is this with you? Do you know that your disposition to commit sin is gone? Look at the sins you used to practice when you were impenitent—how do they appear to you? Do they look pleasant—and would you really love to practice them again if you dared? If you do, if you have the disposition to sin left, you are only convicted. Your *opinions* of sin may be changed, but if the love of that sin remains, as your soul lives, you are still an impenitent sinner.

3. Genuine repentance worketh a reformation of conduct.

I take this idea to be chiefly intended in the text, where it says "Godly sorrow worketh repentance." Godly sorrow produces a reformation of conduct. Otherwise it is a repetition of the same idea; or saying, that repentance produces repentance. Whereas, I suppose the apostle was speaking of such a change of mind as produces a change of conduct, ending in salvation. Now, let me ask you, are you really reformed? Have you forsaken your sins? Or, are you practicing them still? If so, you are still a sinner. However you may have changed your mind, if it has not wrought a change of conduct, an actual reformation, it is not godly repentance, or such as God approve.

4. Repentance, when true and genuine, leads to confession and restitution.

The thief has not repented while he keeps the money he stole. He may have conviction, but no repentance. If he had repentance, he would go and give back the money. If you have cheated any one, and do not restore what you have taken unjustly; or if you have injured any one, and do not set about rectifying the wrong you have done, as far as in you lies, you have not truly repented.

5. True repentance is a permanent change of character and conduct.

The text says it is repentance unto salvation, "not to be repented of." What else does the apostle mean by that expression but this, that true repentance is a change so deep and fundamental that the man never changes back again? People often quote it as if it read, repentance that does not need to be repented of. But that is not what he says. It is not to be repented of; or, in other words, repentance that will not be repented of—so thorough, that there is no going back. The love of sin is truly abandoned. The individual who has truly repented, has so changed his views and feelings, that he will not change back again, or go back to the love of sin. Bear this in mind now, all of you, that the truly penitent sinner exercises feelings of which he never will repent. The text says it is "unto salvation." It goes right on, to the very rest of heaven. The very reason why it ends in salvation is, because it is such as will not be repented of.

And here I cannot but remark, that you see why the doctrine of the Saints' Perseverance is true, and what it means. True repentance is such a thorough change of feelings, and the individual who exercises it comes so to abhor sin, that he will persevere of course, and not go and take back all his repentance and return to sin again.

III. I am to speak of false repentance.

False or spurious repentance is said to be worldly, the sorrow of the world; that is, it is sorrow for sin, arising from worldly considerations and motives connected with the present life, or at most, has respect to his "own happiness" in a future world, and has no regard to the true nature of sin.

1. It is not founded on such a change of opinion as I have specified to belong to true repentance.

The change is not on fundamental points. A person may see the evil consequences of sin in a worldly point of view, and it may fill him with consternation. He may see that it will greatly affect his character, or endanger his life; that if some of his concealed conduct should be found out, he would be disgraced, and this may fill him with fear and distress. It is very common for persons to have this kind of worldly sorrow, when some worldly consideration is at the bottom of it all.

2. False repentance is founded on selfishness.

It may be simply a strong feeling of regret, in the mind of the individual, that he has done as he has, because he sees the evil consequences of it to himself, because it makes him miserable, or exposes him to the wrath of God, or injures his family or his friends, or because it produces some injury to himself in time or in eternity. All this is pure selfishness. He may feel remorse of conscience—biting, consuming *remorse*—and no true repentance. It may extend to fear—deep and dreadful fear—of the wrath of God and the pains of hell, and yet be purely selfish, and all the while there may be no such thing as a hearty abhorrence of sin, and no feelings of the heart going out after the convictions of the understanding, in regard to the infinite evil of sin.

IV. I am to show how this false or spurious repentance may be known.

1. It leaves the feelings unchanged.

It leaves unbroken and unsubdued the disposition to sin in the heart. The feelings as to the nature of sin are not so changed, but that the individual still feels a desire for sin. He abstains from it, not from abhorrence of it, but from dread of the consequences of it.

2. It works death.

It leads to hypocritical concealment. The individual who has exercised true repentance is willing to have it known that he has repented, and willing to have it known that he was a sinner. He who has only false repentance, resorts to excuses and lying to cover his sins, and is ashamed of his repentance. When he is called to the anxious seat, he will cover up his sins by a thousand apologies and excuses, trying to smooth them over, and extenuate their enormity. If he speaks of his past conduct, he always does it in the softest and most favorable terms. You see a constant disposition to cover up his sin. This repentance leads to death. It makes him commit one sin to cover up another. Instead of that ingenuous, open-hearted breaking forth of sensibility and frankness, you see a palavering, smooth-tongued, half-hearted mincing out of something that is intended to answer the purpose of a confession, and yet to confess nothing.

How is it with you? Are you ashamed to have any person talk with you about your sins? Then your sorrow is only a worldly sorrow, and worketh death. How often you see sinners getting out of the way to avoid conversation about their sins, and yet calling themselves anxious inquirers, and expecting to become Christians in that way. The same kind of sorrow is found in hell. No doubt all those wretched inhabitants of the pit wish to get away from the eye of God. No such sorrow is found among the saints in heaven. Their sorrow is open, ingenuous, full and hearty. Such sorrow is not inconsistent with true happiness. The saints are full of happiness, and yet full of deep and undisguised, and gushing sorrow for sin. But this worldly sorrow is ashamed of itself, is mean and miserable, and worketh death.

3. False repentance produces only a partial reformation of conduct.

The reformation that is produced by worldly sorrow extends only to those things of which the individual has been strongly convicted. The heart is not changed. You will see him avoid only those cardinal sins, about which he has been much exercised.

Observe that young convert. If he is deceived, you will find that there is only a partial change in his conduct. He is reformed in certain things, but there are many things which are wrong that he continues to practice. If you become intimately acquainted with him, instead of finding him tremblingly alive to sin every where, and quick to detect it in every thing that is contrary to the spirit of the gospel, you will find him, perhaps, strict and quick-sighted in regard to certain things, but loose in his conduct and lax in his views on other points, and very far from manifesting a Christian spirit in regard to all sin.

4. Ordinarily, the reformation produced by false sorrow is temporary even in those things which are reformed.

The individual is continually relapsing into his old sins. The reason is, the disposition to sin is not gone, it is only checked and restrained by fear, and as soon as he has a hope and is in the church and gets bolstered up so that his fears are allayed, you see him gradually wearing back, and presently returning to his old sins. This was the difficulty with the house of Israel, that made them so constantly return to their idolatry and other sins. They had only worldly sorrow. You see it now everywhere in the church.

Individuals are reformed for a time, and taken into the church, and then relapse into their old sins. They love to call it getting cold in religion, and backsliding, and the like, but the truth is, they always loved sin, and when the occasion offered, they returned to it, as the sow that was washed to her wallowing in the mire, because she was always a sow.

I would you should understand this point thoroughly.— Here is the foundation of all those fits and starts in religion, that you see so much of. People are awakened, and convicted, and by-and-by they get to hope and settle down in false security and then away they go. Perhaps, they may keep so far on their guard as not to be turned out of the church, but the foundations of sins are not broken up, and they return to their old ways. The woman that loved dress loves it still; and gradually returns to her ribands and gewgaws. The man who loved money loves it yet, and soon slides back into his old ways, and dives into business, and pursues the world as eagerly and devotedly as he did before he joined the church.

Go through all the departments of society, and if you find thorough conversions, you will find that their most besetting sins before conversion are farthest from them now. The real convert is least likely to fall into his old besetting sin, because he abhors it most. But if he is deceived and worldly minded, he is always tending back into the same sins. The woman that loves dress comes out again in all her glory, and dashes as she used to do. The fountain of sin was not broken up. They have not purged out iniquity from their heart but they regarded iniquity in their heart all the time.

5. It is a forced reformation.

The reformation produced by a false repentance, is not only a partial reformation, and a temporary reformation, but it is also forced and constrained. The reformation of one who has true repentance is from the heart; he has no longer a disposition to sin. In him the Bible promise is fulfilled. He actually finds that "Wisdom's ways are ways of pleasantness, and all her paths are peace." He experiences that the Saviour's yoke is easy and his burden is light He has felt that God's commandments are not grievous but joyous. More to be desired are they than gold, yea, than much fine gold; sweeter also than honey and the honeycomb. But this spurious kind of repentance is very different: it is a legal repentance, the result of fear and not of love; a selfish repentance, anything but a free, voluntary, hearty change from sin to obedience. You will find, if there are any individuals here that have this kind of repentance, you are conscious that you do not abstain from sin by choice, because you hate it, but from other considerations. It is more through the forbiddings of conscience, or the fear you shall lose your soul, or lose your hope, or lose your character, than from abhorrence of sin or love to duty.

Such persons always need to be crowded up to do duty, with an express passage of scripture, or else they will apologize for sin, and evade duty, and think there is no great harm in doing as they do. The reason is, they love their sins, and if there is not some express command of God which they dare not fly in the face of, they will practise them. Not so with true repentance. If a thing seems contrary to the great law of love, the person who has true repentance will abhor it, and avoid it of course, whether he has an express command of God for it or not. Show me such a man, and I tell you he don't need an express command to make him give up the drinking or making or vending of strong drink. He sees it is contrary to the great law of benevolence, and he truly abhors it, and would no more do it than he would blaspheme God, or steal, or commit any other abomination.

So the man that has true repentance does not need a "Thus saith the Lord," to keep him from oppressing his fellow men, because he would not do anything wrong. How certainly men would abhor any thing of the kind, if they had truly repented of sin.

6. This spurious repentance leads to self-righteousness.

The individual who has this repentance may know that Jesus Christ is the only Saviour of sinners, and may profess to believe on him and to rely on him alone for salvation, but after all, he is actually placing ten times more reliance on his reformation than on Jesus Christ for his salvation. And if he would watch his own heart, he would know it is so. He may say he expects salvation by Christ, but in fact he is dwelling more on his reformation, and his hope is founded more on that, than on the atonement of Christ, and he is really patching up a righteousness of his own.

7. It leads to false security.

The individual supposes the worldly sorrow he has had to be true repentance, and he trusts to it. It is a curious fact, that so far as I have been able to get at the state of mind of this class of persons, they seem to take it for granted that Christ will save them because they have had sorrow on account of their sins, although they are not conscious that they have ever felt any resting in Christ. They felt sorrow, and then they got relief and felt better, and now they expect to be saved by Christ, when their very consciousness will teach them that they have never felt a hearty reliance on Christ.

8. It hardens the heart.

The individual who has this kind of sorrow becomes harder in heart, in proportion to the number of times that he exercises such sorrow. If he has strong emotions of conviction, and his heart does not break up and flow out, the fountains of feeling are more and more dried up, and his heart more and more difficult to be reached. Take a real Christian, one who has truly repented, and every time you bring the truth to bear upon him so as to break him down before God, he becomes more and more mellow, and more easily affected, and excited, and melted, and broken down under God's blessed word, so long as he lives—and to all eternity. His heart gets into the habit of going along with the convictions of his understanding, and he becomes as teachable and tractable as a little child.

Here is the grand distinction. Let churches, or individual members, who have only this worldly repentance, pass through a revival, and get waked up, and bustle about, and then grow cold again. Let this be repeated and you find them more and more difficult to be roused, till by-and-by they become as hard as the nether mill-stone, and nothing can ever rally them to a revival again. Directly over against this are those churches and individuals who have true repentance. Let them go through successive revivals, and you find them growing more and more mellow and tender until they get to such a state, that if they hear the trumpet blow for a revival, they kindle and glow instantly, and are ready for the work.

This distinction is as broad as between light and darkness. It is every where observable among the churches and church members. You see the principle illustrated in sinners, who, after passing through repeated revivals, by-and-by will scoff and rail at all religion, and although the heavens hang with clouds of mercy over their heads, they heed it not, but reject it. It is so in churches and members; if they have not true repentance, every fresh excitement hardens the heart and renders them more difficult to be reached by the truth.

9. It sears the conscience.

Such persons are liable at first to be thrown into distress, whenever the truth is flashed upon their mind. They may not have so much conviction as the real Christian. But the real Christian is filled with peace at the very time that his tears are flowing from conviction of sin. And each repeated season of conviction makes him more and more watchful, and tender, and careful, till his conscience becomes, like the apple of his eye, so tender that the very appearance of evil will offend it. But the other kind of sorrow, which does not lead to hearty renunciation of sin, leaves the heart harder than before, and by-and-by sears the conscience as with a hot iron. This sorrow worketh death.

10. It rejects Jesus Christ as the ground of hope.

Depending on reformation and sorrow, or any thing else, it leads to no such reliance on Jesus Christ, that the love of Christ will constrain him to labor all his days for Christ.

11. It is transient and temporary.

This kind of repentance is sure to be repented of. By-and-by you will find such persons becoming ashamed of the deep feelings that they had. They do not want to speak of them, and if they talk of them it is always lightly and coldly. They perhaps hustled about in time of revival, and appeared as much engaged as any body, and very likely were among the extremes in every thing that was done. But now the revival is over, and you find them opposed to new measures, and changing back, and ashamed of their zeal. They in fact repent of their repentance.

Such persons, after they have joined the church, will be ashamed of having come to the anxious seat. When the height of the revival has gone by, they will begin to talk against being too enthusiastic, and the necessity of getting into a more sober and consistent way in religion. Here is the secret—they had a repentance of which they afterwards repented.

You sometimes find persons who profess to be converted in a revival, turning against the very measures, and means, and doctrines, by which they profess to have been converted. Not so with the true Christian. He is never ashamed of his repentance. The last thing he would ever think of being ashamed of, is the excitement of feeling he felt in a revival.

CONCLUSION

1. We learn from what has been said, one reason why there is so much spasmodic religion in the church.

They have mistaken conviction for conversion, the sorrow of the world for that godly sorrow that worketh repentance unto salvation, not to be repented of. I am convinced, after years of observation, that here is the true reason for the present deplorable state of the church all over the land.

2. We see why sinners under conviction feel as if it was a great cross to become Christians.

They think it a great trial to give up their ungodly companions, and to give up their sins. Whereas, if they had true repentance, they would not think it any cross to give up their sins. I recollect how I used to feel, when I first saw young persons becoming Christians and joining the church. I thought it was a good thing on the whole to have religion, because they would save their souls and get to heaven. But for the time, it seemed to be a very sorrowful thing. I never dreamed then that these young people could be really happy now. I believe it is very common for persons, who know that religion is good on the whole, and good in the end, to think they cannot be happy in religion. This is all owing to a mistake respecting the true nature of repentance. They do not understand that true repentance leads to an abhorrence of those things that were formerly loved. Sinners do not see that when their young friends become true Christians, they feel an abhorrence for their balls and parties, and sinful amusements and follies, that the love for these things is crucified.

I once knew a young lady who was converted to God. Her father was a very proud worldly man. She used to be very fond of dress, and the dancing school, and balls. After she was converted, her father would force her to go to the dancing school. He used to go along with her, and force her to stand up and dance. She would go there and weep, and sometimes when she was standing up on the floor to dance, her feelings of abhorrence and sorrow would so come over her, that she would turn away and burst into tears. Here you see the cause of all that. She truly repented of these things, with a repentance not to be repented of. O, how many associations would such a scene recall to a Christian, what compassion for her former gay companions, what abhorrence of their giddy mirth, how she longed to be in the prayer-meeting, how could she be happy there? Such is the mistake which the impenitent, or those who have only worldly sorrow, fall into, in regard to the happiness of the real Christian.

3. Here you see what is the matter with those professing Christians who think it a cross to be very strict in religion.

Such persons are always apologising for their sins, and pleading for certain practices, that are not consistent with strict religion. It shows that they love sin still, and will go as far as they dare in it. If they were true Christians, they would abhor it, and turn from it, and would feel it to be a cross to be dragged to it.

4. You see the reason why some know not what it is to enjoy religion.

They are not cheerful and happy in religion. They are grieved because they have to break off from so many things they love, or because they have to give so much money.

They are in the fire all the time. Instead of rejoicing in every opportunity of self-denial, and rejoicing in the plainest and most cutting exhibitions of truth, it is a great trial to them to be told their duty, when it crosses their inclinations and habits. The plain truth distresses them. Why? Because their hearts do not love to do duty. If they loved to do their duty, every ray of light that broke in upon their minds from heaven, pointing out their duty, would be welcomed, and make them more and more happy.

Whenever you see such persons, if they feel cramped and distressed because the truth presses them, if their hearts do not yield and go along with the truth, *hypocrite* is the name of all such professors of religion. If you find that they are distressed like anxious sinners, and that the more you point out their sins the more they are distressed, be you sure, that they have never truly repented of their sins, nor given themselves up to be God's.

5. You see why many professed converts, who have had very deep exercises at the time of their conversion, afterwards apostatize.

They had deep convictions and great distress of mind, and afterwards they got relief and their joy was very great, and they were amazingly happy for a season. But by-and-by they decline, and then they apostatize. Some, who do not discriminate properly between true and false repentance, and who think there cannot be such "deep" exercises without divine power, call these cases of falling from grace. But the truth is, They went out from us because they were not of us. They never had that repentance that kills and annihilates the disposition to sin.

6. See why backsliders are so miserable.

Perhaps you will infer that I suppose all true Christians are perfect, from what I said about the disposition to sin being broken up and changed. But this does not follow. There is a radical difference between a backslidden Christian and a hypocrite who has gone back from his profession. The hypocrite loves the world, and enjoys sin when he returns to it. He may have some fears and some remorse, and some apprehension about the loss of character; but after all he enjoys sin. Not so with the backslidden Christian. He loses his first love, then he falls a prey to temptation, and so he goes into sin. But he does not love it; it is always bitter to him; he feels unhappy and away from home. He has indeed, at the time, no Spirit of God, no love of God in exercise to keep him from sin, but he does not love sin; he is unhappy in sin; he feels that he is a wretch. He is as different from the hypocrite as can be. Such an one, when he leaves the love of God, may be delivered over to Satan for a time, for the destruction of the flesh, that the Spirit may be saved; but he can never again enjoy sin as he used to, or delight himself as he once could in the pleasures of the world. Never again can he drink in iniquity like water. So long as he continues to wander, he is a wretch. If there is one such here to-night, you know it.

7. You see why convicted sinners are afraid to pledge themselves to give up their sins.

They tell you they dare not promise to do it, because they are afraid they shall not keep the promise. There you have the reason. "They love sin." The drunkard knows that he loves rum, and though he may be constrained to keep his promise and abstain from it, yet his appetite still craves it. And so with the convicted sinner. He feels that he loves sin, that his hold on sin has never been broken off, and he dares not promise.

8. See why some professors of religion are so much opposed to pledges.

It is on the same principle. They love their sins so well, they know their hearts will plead for indulgence, and they are afraid to promise to give them up. Hence many who profess to think they are Christians, refuse to join the church. The secret reason is, they feel that their heart is still going after sin, and they dare not come under the obligations of the church-covenant. They do not want to be subject to the discipline of the church, in case they should sin. That man knows he is a hypocrite.

9. Those sinners who have worldly sorrow, can now see where the difficulty lies, and what is the reason they are not converted.

Their intellectual views of sin may be such, that if their hearts corresponded, they would be Christians. And perhaps they are thinking that this is true repentance. But if they were truly willing to give up sin, and all sin, they would not hesitate to pledge themselves to it, and to have all the world know that they had done it. If there are any such here, I ask you now to come forward, and take these seats. If you are willing to give up sin, you are willing to promise to do it, and willing to have it known that you have done it. But if you resist conviction, and when your understanding is enlightened to see what you ought to do, your heart still goeth forth after your sins, tremble, sinner, at the prospect before you. All your convictions will avail you nothing. They will only sink you deeper in hell for having resisted them.

If you are willing to give up your sins, you can signify it as I have named. But if you still love your sins, and want to retain them, you can keep your seats. And now, shall we go and tell God in prayer, that these sinners are unwilling to give up their sins, that though they are convinced they are wrong, they love their idols, and after them they will go? The Lord have mercy on them, for they are in a fearful case.

2

TRUE AND FALSE CONVERSION

Behold all ye that kindle a fire, that compass yourselves about with sparks ;
walk in the light of your fire, and in the sparks that ye have kindled. This
shall ye have of my hand ; ye shall lie down in sorrow.—Isaiah 50. 11

IT is evident, from the connection of these words in the
chapter, that the prophet was addressing those who
professed to be religious, and who flattered themselves that
they were in a state of salvation, but in fact their hope was
a fire of their own kindling, and sparks created by themselves. Before I proceed to discuss the subject, let me
say that as I have given notice that it was my intention to
discuss the nature of true and false conversion, it will be
of no use but to those who will be honest in applying it to
themselves. If you mean to profit by the discourse, you
must resolve to make a faithful application of it to yourselves—just as honest as if you thought you were now
going to the solemn judgment. If you will do this, I may
hope to be able to lead you to discover your true state,
and if you are now deceived, direct you in the true path
to salvation. If you will not do this, I shall preach in vain,
and you will hear in vain.

I design to show the difference between true and false
conversion, and shall take up the subject in the following
order :

I. Show that the natural state of man is a state of pure
selfishness.

II. Show that the character of the converted is that of
benevolence.

III. That the new birth consists in a change from selfishness to benevolence.

IV. Point out some things wherein saints and sinners, or true and spurious converts, may agree, and some things in which they differ.

V. Answer some objections that may be offered against the view I have taken, and conclude with some remarks.

1. I am to show that the natural state of man, or that in which all men are found before conversion, is pure, unmingled selfishness.

By which I mean, that they have no gospel benevolence. Selfishness is regarding one's own happiness supremely, and seeking one's own good because it is his own. He who is selfish places his own happiness above other interests of greater value; such as the glory of God and the good of the universe. That mankind, before conversion, are in this state, is evident from many considerations.

Every man knows that all other men are selfish. All the dealings of mankind are conducted on this principle. If any man overlooks this, and undertakes to deal with mankind as if they were not selfish, but were disinterested, he will be thought deranged.

II. In a converted state, the character is that of benevolence.

An individual who is converted is benevolent, and not supremely selfish. Benevolence is loving the happiness of others, or rather choosing the happiness of others. Benevolence is a compound word, that properly signifies good willing, or choosing the happiness of others. This is God's state of mind. We are told that God is love; that is, he is benevolent. Benevolence comprises his whole character. All his moral attributes are only so many modifications of benevolence. An individual who is converted is in this respect like God. I do not mean to be understood, that no one is converted, unless he is purely and perfectly benevolent, as God is; but that the balance of his mind, his prevailing choice is benevolent. He sincerely seeks the good of others, for its own sake. And, by disinterested benevolence I do not mean, that a person who is disinterested feels no interest in his object of pursuit, but that he seeks the happiness of others for its own sake, and not for the sake of its reaction on himself, in promoting his own happiness. He chooses to do good because he rejoices in the happiness of others, and desires their happiness for its own sake. God is purely and disinterestedly benevolent. He does not make his creatures happy for the sake of thereby promoting his own happiness, but because he loves their happiness and chooses it for its own sake. Not that he does not feel happy in promoting the happiness of his creatures, but that he does not do it for the sake of his own gratification. The man who is disinterested feels happy in doing good. Otherwise doing good itself would not be virtue in him. In other words, if he did not love to do good, and enjoy doing good, it would not be virtue in him.

Benevolence is holiness. It is what the law of God requires : " Thou shalt love the Lord thy God, with all thy heart and soul and strength, and thy neighbor as thyself." Just as certainly as the converted man yields obedience to the law of God, and just as certainly as he is like God, he is benevolent. It is the leading feature of his character, that he is seeking the happiness of others, and not his own nappiness, as his supreme end.

III. That true conversion is a change from a state of supreme selfishness to benevolence.

It is a change in the end of pursuit, and not a mere change in the means of attaining the end. It is not true that the converted and the unconverted differ only in the means they use, while both are aiming at the same end It is not true that Gabriel and Satan are pursuing the same end, and both alike aiming at their own happiness, only pursuing a different way. Gabriel does not obey God for the sake of promoting his own happiness. A man may change his means, and yet have the same end, his own happiness. He may do good for the sake of the temporal benefit. He may not believe in religion, or in any eternity, and yet may see that doing good will be for his advantage in this world. Suppose, then, that his eyes are opened, and he sees the reality of eternity; and then he may take up religion as a means of happiness in eternity. Now, every one can see that there is no virtue in this. It is the design that gives character to the act, not the means employed to effect the design. The true and the false convert differ in this. The true convert chooses, as the end of his pursuit, the glory of God and the good of his kingdom. This end he chooses for its own sake, because he views this as the greatest good, as a greater good than his own individual happiness. Not that he is indifferent to his own happiness, but he prefers God's glory, because it is a greater good. He looks on the happiness of every individual according to its real importance, as far as he is capable of valuing it, and he chooses the greatest good as his supreme object.

IV. Now I am to show some things in which true saints and deceived persons may agree, and some things in which they differ.

1. They may agree in leading a strictly moral life.

The difference is in their motives. The true saint leads a moral life from love to holiness; the deceived person from selfish considerations. He uses morality as a means to an end, to effect his own happiness. The true saint loves it as an end.

2. They may be equally prayerful, so far as the form of praying is concerned.

The difference is in their motives. The true saint loves to pray; the other prays because he hopes to derive some benefit to himself from praying. The true saint expects a benefit from praying, but that is not his leading motive. The other prays from no other motive.

3. They may be equally zealous in religion.

One may have great zeal, because his zeal is according to knowledge, and he sincerely desires and loves to promote religion, for its own sake. The other may show equal zeal, for the sake of having his own salvation more assured, and because he is afraid of going to hell if he does not work for the Lord, or to quiet his conscience, and not because he loves religion for its own sake.

4. They may be equally conscientious in the discharge of duty ; the true convert because he loves to do duty, and the other because he dare not neglect it.

5. Both may pay equal regard to what is right; the true convert because he loves what is right, and the other because he knows he cannot be saved unless he does right. He is honest in his common business transactions, because it is the only way to secure his own interest. Verily, they have their reward. They get the reputation of being honest among men, but if they have no higher motive, they will have no reward from God.

6. They may agree in their desires, in many respects. They may agree in their desires to serve God ; the true convert because he loves the service of God, and the deceived person for the reward, as the hired servant serves his master.

They may agree in their desires to be useful ; the true convert desiring usefulness for its own sake, the deceived person because he knows that is the way to obtain the favor of God. And then in proportion as he is awakened to the importance of having God's favor, will be the intensity of his desires to be useful.

In desires for the conversion of souls ; the true saint because it will glorify God ; the deceived person to gain the favor of God. He will be actuated in this, just as he is in giving money. Who ever doubted that a person might give his money to the Bible Society, or the Mission-ary Society, from selfish motives alone, to procure happi-ness, or applause, or obtain the favor of God? He may just as well desire the conversion of souls, and labor to promote it, from motives purely selfish.

To glorify God; the true saint because he loves to see God glorified, and the deceived person because he know that is the way to be saved. The true convert has hi heart set on the glory of God, as his great end, and he de sires to glorify God as an end, for its own sake. The other desires it as a means to *his* great end, the benefit of him-self.

To repent. The true convert abhors sin on account of its hateful nature, because it dishonors God, and there-fore he desires to repent of it. The other desires to repent, because he knows that unless he does repent he will be damned.

To believe in Jesus Christ. The true saint desires it to glorify God, and because he loves the truth for its own sake. The other desires to believe, that he may have a stronger hope of going to heaven.

To obey God. The true saint that he may increase in holiness; the false professor because he desires the rewards of obedience.

7. They may agree not only in their desires, but in their resolutions. They may both resolve to give up sin, and to obey God, and to lay themselves out in promoting religion, and building up the kingdom of Christ; and they may both resolve it with great strength of purpose, but with different motives.

8. They may also agree in their designs. They may both really design to glorify God, and to convert men, and to extend the kingdom of Christ, and to have the world converted; the true saint from love to God and

holiness, and the other for the sake of securing his own happiness. One chooses it as an end, the other as a means to promote a selfish end.

They may both design to be truly holy; the true saint because he loves holiness, and the deceived person because he knows that he can be happy in no other way.

9. They may agree not only in their desires, and resolutions and designs, but also in their affection towards many objects.

They may both love the Bible; the true saint because it is God's truth, and he delights in it, and feasts his soul on it; the other because he thinks it is in his own favor, and is the charter of his own hopes.

They may both love God; the one because he sees God's character to be supremely excellent and lovely in itself and he loves it for its own sake; the other because he thinks God is his particular friend, that is going to make him happy for ever, and he connects the idea of God with his own interest.

They may both love Christ. The true convert loves his character; the deceived person thinks he will save *him* from hell, and give him eternal life—and why should he not love him?

They may both love Christians: the true convert because he sees in them the image of Christ, and the deceived person because they belong to his own denomination, or because they are on his side, and he feels the same interest and hopes with them.

10. They may also agree in hating the same things. They may both hate infidelity, and oppose it strenuously —the true saint because it is opposed to God and holiness, and the deceived person because it injures an interest in which he is deeply concerned, and if true, destroys all his own hopes for eternity. So they may hate error; one because it is detestable in itself, and contrary to God—

and the other because it is contrary to his views and opinions.

I recollect seeing in writing, some time ago, an attack on a minister for publishing certain opinions, " because," said the writer, "these sentiments would destroy all *my hopes* for eternity." A very good reason indeed ! as good as a selfish being needs for opposing an opinion.

They may both hate sin ; the true convert because it is odious to God, and the deceived person because it is injurious to himself. Cases have occurred, where an individual has hated his own sins, and yet not forsaken them. How often the drunkard, as he looks back at what he once was, and contrasts his present degradation with what he might have been, abhors his drink ; not for its own sake, but because it has ruined him. And he still loves his cups, and continues to drink, though, when he looks at their effects, he feels indignation.

They may be both opposed to sinners. The opposition of true saints is a benevolent opposition, viewing and abhorring their character and conduct, as calculated to subvert the kingdom of God. The other is opposed to sinners because they are opposed to the religion he has espoused, and because they are not on his side.

11. So they may both rejoice in the same things. Both may rejoice in the prosperity of Zion, and the conversion of souls ; the true convert because he has his heart set on it, and loves it for its own sake, as the greatest good, and the deceived person because that particular thing in which he thinks he has such a great interest is advancing.

12. Both may mourn and feel distressed at the low state of religion in the church : the true convert because God is dishonored, and the deceived person because his own soul is not happy, or because religion is not in favor.

Both may love the society of the saints ; the true convert because his soul enjoys their spiritual conversation, the other because he hopes to derive some advantage from their company.   The first enjoys it because out of the abundance of the heart the mouth speaketh ; the other because he loves to talk about the great interest he feels in religion, and the hope he has of going to heaven.

13. Both may love to attend religious meetings ; the true saint because his heart delights in acts of worship, in prayer and praise, in hearing the word of God and in communion with God and his saints, and the other because he thinks a religious meeting a good place to prop up his hope.   He may have a hundred reasons for loving them, and yet not at all for their own sake, or because he loves in itself, the worship and the service of God.

14. Both may find pleasure in the duties of the closet. The true saint loves his closet, because he draws near to God, and finds delight in communion with God, where there are no embarrassments to keep him from going right to God and conversing.   The deceived person finds a kind of satisfaction in it, because it is his duty to pray in secret and he feels a self-righteous satisfaction in doing it.   Nay he may feel a certain pleasure in it, from a kind of excite ment of the mind which he mistakes for communion with God.

15. They may both love the doctrines of grace ; the true saint because they are so glorious to God, the other because he thinks them a guarantee of his own salvation.

16. They may both love the precept of God's law ; the true saint because it is so excellent, so holy, and just, and good ; the other because he thinks it will make him happy if he loves it, and he does it as a means of happiness.

Both may consent to the penalty of the law.   The true saint consents to it in his own case, because he feels it to be just in itself for God to send him to hell.   The deceived person because he thinks *he* is in no danger from it.   He feels a respect for it, because he knows that it is right, and his conscience approves it, but he has never consented to it in his own case.

17. They may be equally liberal in giving to benevolent societies. None of you doubt that two men may give equal sums to a benevolent object, but from totally different motives. One gives to do good, and would be just as willing to give as not, if he knew that no other living person would give. The other gives for the credit of it, or to quiet his conscience, or because he hopes to purchase the favor of God.

18. They may be equally self-denying in many things. Self-denial is not confined to true saints. Look at the sacrifices and self-denials of the Mohammedans, going on their pilgrimage to Mecca. Look at the heathen, throwing themselves under the car of Juggernaut. Look at the poor ignorant papists, going up and down over the sharp stones on their bare knees, till they stream with blood. A protestant congregation will not contend that there is any religion in that. But is there not self-denial? The true saint denies himself, for the sake of doing more good to others. He is more set on this than on his own indulgence or his own interest. The deceived person may go equal lengths, but from purely selfish motives.

19. They may both be willing to suffer martyrdom. Read the lives of the martyrs, and you will have no doubt that some were willing to suffer, from a wrong idea of the rewards of martyrdom, and would rush upon their own destruction because they were persuaded it was the sure road to eternal life.

In all these cases, the motives of one class are directly over against the other. The difference lies in the choice of different *ends*. One chooses his own interest, the other chooses God's interest, as his chief end. For a person to pretend that both these classes are aiming at the same end, is to say that an impenitent sinner is just as benevolent as a real Christian ; or that a Christian is not benevolent like God, but is only seeking his own happiness, and seeking it in religion rather than in the world.

And here is the proper place to answer an inquiry, which is often made : " If these two classes of persons may be alike in so many particulars, how are we to know our own real character, or to tell to which class we belong ? We know that the heart is deceitful above all things, and desperately wicked, and how are we to know whether we love God and holiness for their own sake, or whether we are seeking the favor of God, and aiming at heaven for our own benefit ?" I answer,

1. If we are truly benevolent, it will appear in our daily transactions. This character, if real, will show itself in our business, if anywhere. If selfishness rules our conduct there, as sure as God reigns we are truly selfish. If in our dealings with men we are selfish, we are so in our dealings with God. " For whoso loveth not his brother, whom he hath seen, how can he love God, whom he hath not seen ?" Religion is not merely love to God, but love to man also. And if our daily transactions show us to be selfish, we are unconverted ; or else benevolence is not essential to religion, and a man can be religious without loving his neighbor as himself.

2. If you are disinterested in religion, religious duties will not be a task to you. You will not go about religion as the laboring man goes to his toil, for the sake of a living. The laboring man takes pleasure in his labor, but it is not for its own sake. He would not do it if he could help it. In its own nature it is a task, and if he takes any pleasure in it, it is for its anticipated results, the support and comfort of his family, or the increase of his property.

Precisely such is the state of some persons in regard to religion. They go to it as the sick man takes his medicine, because they desire its effects, and they know they must have it or perish.   It is a task that they never would do for its own sake.   Suppose men love labor, as a child loves play.   They would do it all day long, and never be tired of doing it, without any other inducement than the pleasure in doing it.   So it is in religion, where it is loved for its own sake, there is no weariness in it.

3. If selfishness is the prevailing character of your religion, it will take sometimes one form and sometimes another.   For instance : If it is a time of general coldness in the church, real converts will still enjoy their own secret communion with God, although there may not be so much doing to attract notice in public.   But the deceived person will then invariably be found driving after the world. Now, let the true saints rise up, and make a noise, and speak their joys aloud, so that religion begins to be talked of again ; and perhaps the deceived professor will soon begin to bustle about, and appear to be even more zealous than the true saint.   He is impelled by his convictions and not affections.   When there is no public interest, he feels no conviction ; but when the church awakes, he is convicted, and compelled to stir about, to keep his conscience quiet. It is only selfishness in another form.

4. If you are selfish, your enjoyment in religion will depend mainly on the strength of your hopes of heaven, and not on the exercise of your affections.   Your enjoyments are not in the employments of religion themselves, but of a vastly different kind from those of the true saint.   They are mostly from anticipating.   When your evidences are renewed, and you feel very certain of going to heaven, then you enjoy religion a good deal.   It depends on your hope, and not on your love for the things for which you hope. You hear persons tell of their having no enjoyment in religion when they lose their hopes.   The reason is plain. If they loved religion for its own sake, their enjoyment would not depend on their hope.   A person who loves his

employments is happy anywhere. And if you loved the employments of religion, you would be happy if God should put you in hell, provided he would only let you employ yourself in religion. If you might pray and praise God, you would feel that you could be happy anywhere in the universe ; for you would still be doing the things in which your happiness mainly consists. If the duties of religion are not the things in which you feel enjoyment, and if all your enjoyment depends on your hope, you have no true religion ; it is all selfishness.

I do not say that true saints do not enjoy their hope. But that is not the great thing with them. They think very little about their own hopes. Their thoughts are employed about something else. The deceived person, on the contrary, is sensible that he does not enjoy the duties of religion ; but only that the more he does, the more confident he is of heaven. He takes only such kind of enjoyment in it, as a man does who thinks that by great labor he shall have great wealth.

5. If you are selfish in religion, your enjoyments will oe chiefly from anticipation. The true saint already enjoys the peace of God, and has heaven begun in his soul. He has not merely the prospect of it, but eternal life actually begun in him. He has that faith which is the very substance of things hoped for. Nay, he has the very feelings of heaven in him. He anticipates joys higher in degree, but the same in kind. He knows that he has heaven begun in him, and is not obliged to wait till he dies to taste the joys of eternal life. His enjoyment is in proportion to his holiness, and not in proportion to his hope.

6. Another difference by which it may be known whether you are selfish in religion, is this—that the deceived person has only a purpose of obedience, and the other has a preference of obedience. This is an important distinction, and I fear few persons make it. Multitudes

have a purpose of obedience, who have no true preference of obedience. Preference is actual choice, or obedience of heart. You often hear individuals speak of their having had a purpose to do this or that act of obedience, but failed to do it. And they will tell you how difficult it is to execute their purpose. The true saint, on the other hand, really prefers, and in his heart chooses obedience, and therefore he finds it easy to obey. The one has a purpose to obey, like that which Paul had before he was converted, as he tells us in the seventh chapter of Romans. He had a strong purpose of obedience, but did not obey, because his heart was not in it. The true convert prefers obedience for its own sake ; he actually chooses it, and does it. The other purposes to be holy, because he knows that is the only way to be happy. The true saint chooses holiness for its own sake, and he is holy.

7. The true convert and the deceived person also differ in their faith. The true saint has a confidence in the general character of God, that leads him to unqualified submission to God. A great deal is said about the kinds of faith, but without much meaning. True confidence in the Lord's special promises, depends on confidence in God's general character. There are only two principles on which any government, human or divine, is obeyed, fear and confidence. No matter whether it is the government of a family, or a ship, or a nation, or a universe. All obedience springs from one of these two principles. In the one case, individuals obey from hope of reward and fear of the penalty. In the other, from that confidence in the character of the government, which works by love. One child obeys his parent from confidence in his parent. He has faith which works by love. The other yields an outward obedience from hope and fear. The true convert has this faith, or confidence in God, that leads him to obey God because he loves God. This is the obedience of faith.

He has that confidence in God, that he submits himself wholly into the hands of God.

The other has only a partial faith, and only a partial submission. The devil has a partial faith. He believes and trembles. A person may believe that Christ came to save sinners, and on that ground may submit to him, to be saved ; while he does not submit wholly to him, to be governed and disposed of. His submission is only on condition that he shall be saved. It is never with that unreserved confidence in God's whole character, that leads him to say, " Thy will be done." He only submits to be saved. His religion is the religion of law. The other is gospel religion. One is selfish, the other benevolent. Here lies the true difference between the two classes. The religion of one is outward and hypocritical. The other is that of the heart holy, and acceptable to God.

8, I will only mention one difference more. If your religion is selfish, you will rejoice particularly in the conversion of sinners, where your own agency is concerned in it, but will have very little satisfaction in it, where it is through the agency of others. The selfish person rejoices when he is active and successful in converting sinners, because he thinks he shall have a great reward. But instead of delighting in it when done by others, he will be even envious. The true saint sincerely delights to have others useful, and rejoices when sinners are converted by the instrumentality of others as much as if it was his own. There are some who will take interest in a revival, only so far as themselves are connected with it, while it would seem they had rather sinners should remain unconverted, than that they should be saved by the instrumentality of an evangelist, or a minister of another denomination. The true spirit of a child of God is to say, " Send, Lord, by whom thou wilt send—only let souls be saved, and thy name glorified !"

V. I am to answer some objections which are **made** against this view of the subject.

Objection 1. " Am I not to have any regard to my own happiness ? "

Answer. It is right to regard your own happiness according to its relative value. Put it in this scale, by the side of the glory of God and the good of the universe, and then decide, and give it the value which belongs to it. This is precisely what God does. And this is what he means, when he commands you to love your neighbor as yourself.

And again—You will in fact promote your own happiness, precisely in proportion as you leave it out of view. Your happiness will be in proportion to your disinterestedness. True happiness consists mainly in the gratification of virtuous desires. There may be pleasure in gratifying desires that are selfish, but it is not real happiness. But to be virtuous, your desires must be disinterested. Suppose a man sees a beggar in the street ; there he sits on the curbstone, cold and hungry, without friends, and ready to perish. The man's feelings are touched, and he steps into a grocery close by, and buys him a loaf of bread. At once the countenance of the beggar lights up, and he looks unutterable gratitude. Now it is plain to be seen that the gratification of the man in the act is precisely in proportion to the singleness of his motive. If he did it purely and solely out of benevolence, his gratification is complete in the act itself. But if he did it, partly to make it known that he is a charitable and humane person, then his happiness is not complete until the deed is published to others. Suppose here is a sinner in his sins ; he is truly wicked and truly wretched. Your compassion is excited, and you convert and save him. If your motives were to obtain honor among men, and to secure the favor of God, you are not completely happy until the deed is told, and perhaps put

in the newspaper.   But if you wished purely to save a soul
from death, then as soon as you see that done, your gratification is complete and your joy unmingled.   So it is in all
religious duties ; your happiness is precisely in proportion
as you are disinterested.

If you aim at doing good for its own sake, then you
will be happy in proportion as you do good.   But if you
aim directly at your own happiness, and if you do good
simply as a means of securing your own happiness, you
will fail.   You will be like the child pursuing his own
shadow ; he can never overtake it, because it always keeps
just so far before him.   Suppose in the case I have mentioned, you have no desire to relieve the beggar, but regard
simply the applause of a certain individual.   Then you will
feel no pleasure at all in the relief of the beggar ; but when
that individual hears of it and commends it, then you are
gratified.   But you are not gratified in the thing itself.
Or suppose you aim at the conversion of sinners ; but if it
is not love to sinners that leads you to do it, how can the
conversion of sinners make you happy ?   It has no tendency to gratify the desire that prompted the effort.   The
truth is, God has so constituted the mind of man, that it
must seek the happiness of others as its end or it cannot
be happy.   Here is the true reason why all the world, seeking their own happiness, and not the happiness of others,
fail of their end.   It is always just so far before them.   If
they would leave off seeking their own happiness, and lay
themselves out to do good, they would be happy.

Objection 2. "Did not Christ regard the joy set before him ?   And did not Moses also have respect unto the
recompense of reward ?   And does not the Bible say we
love God because he first loved us."

Answer 1. It is true that Christ despised the shame
and endured the cross, and had regard to the joy set before him.   But what was the joy set before him ?   Not

his own salvation, not his own happiness, but the **great** good he would do in the salvation of the world. He **was** perfectly happy in himself. But the happiness of others was what he aimed at. This was the joy set before him. And that he obtained.

Answer 2. So Moses had respect to the recompense **of** reward. But was that his own comfort ? Far from it. The recompense of reward was the salvation of the people of Israel. What did he say ? When God proposed to destroy the nation, and make of him a great nation, had Moses been selfish he would have said, " That is right, Lord ; be it unto thy servant according to thy word." But what does he say ? Why, his heart was so set on the salvation of his people, and the glory of God, that he would not think of it for a moment, but said, " If thou wilt, forgive their sin ; and if not, blot me I pray thee out of thy book, which thou hast written." And in another case, when God said he would destroy them, and make of Moses a greater and a mightier nation, Moses thought of God's glory, and said, " Then the Egyptians shall hear of it, and all the nations will say, Because the Lord was not able to bring this people into the land." He could not bear to think of having his own interest exalted at the expense of God's glory. It was really a greater reward, to his benevolent mind, to have God glorified, and the children of Israel saved, than any personal advantage whatever to himself could be.

Answer 3. Where it is said, " We love him because he first loved us " the language plainly bears two interpretations ; either that his love to us has provided the way for our return and the influence that brought us to love him, or that we love him for his favor shown to ourselves.— That the latter is not the meaning is evident, because Jesus Christ has so expressly reprobated the principle, in his sermon on the mount : " If ye love them which love you, what thank have ye ? Do not the publicans the same ?" If we love God, not for his character but for his favors to us, Jesus Christ has written us reprobate.

Objection 3. "Does not the Bible offer happiness as the reward of virtue ?"

Answer. The Bible speaks of happiness as the result of virtue, but no where declares virtue to consist in the pursuit of one's own happiness. The Bible is every where inconsistent with this, and represents virtue to consist in doing good to others. We can see by the philosophy of the mind, that it must be so. If a person desires the good of others, he will be happy in proportion as he gratifies that desire. Happiness is the result of virtue, but virtue does not consist in the direct pursuit of one's own happiness, but is wholly inconsistent with it.

Objection 4. "God aims at our happiness, and shall we be more benevolent than God ? Should we not be like God ? May we not aim at the same thing that God aims at ? Should we not be seeking the same end that God seeks ?"

Answer. This objection is specious, but futile and rotten. God is benevolent to others. He aims at the happiness of others, and at our happiness. And to be like him, we must aim at, that is, delight in his happiness and glory, and the honor and glory of the universe, according to their real value.

Objection 5. "Why does the Bible appeal continually to the hopes and fears of men, if a regard to our own happiness is not a proper motive to action ?"

Answer 1. The Bible appeals to the constitutional susceptibilities of men, not to their selfishness. Man dreads harm, and it is not wrong to avoid it. We may have a due regard to our own happiness, according to its value.

Answer 2. And again ; mankind are so besotted with sin, that God cannot get their attention to consider his true character, and the reasons for loving him, unless he appeals to their hopes and fears. But when they are awakened, then he presents the gospel to them. When a minister has preached the terrors of the Lord till he has got his hearers alarmed and aroused, so that they will give attention, he has gone far enough in that line ; and then he ought to spread out all the character of God before them, to engage their hearts to love him for his own excellence.

Objection 6. " Do not the inspired writers say, Repent, and believe the gospel, and you shall be saved ?"

Answer. Yes ; but they require "true" repentance ; that is, to forsake sin because it is hateful in itself. It is not true repentance, to forsake sin on condition of pardon, or to say, " I will be sorry for my sins, if you will forgive me." So they require true faith, and true submission·; not conditional faith, or partial submission. This is what the Bible insists on. It says he shall be saved, but it must oe disinterested repentance, and disinterested submission.

Objection 7. " Does not the gospel hold out pardon as a motive to submission."

Answer. This depends on the sense in which you use the term *motive*. If you mean that God spreads out before men his whole character, and the whole truth of the case, as reasons to engage the sinner's love and repentance, I say, Yes ; his compassion, and willingness to pardon, are reasons for loving God, because they are a part of his glorious excellence, which we are bound to love. But if you mean by " motive" a condition, and that the sinner is to repent on condition he shall be pardoned. then I say, that the Bible no where holds out any such view of the matter. It never authorizes a sinner to say, " I will repent *if* you will forgive," and no where offers pardon as a motive to repentance, in such a sense as this.

With two short remarks I will close.

1. We see, from this subject, why it is that professors of religion have such different views or the nature of the gospel.

Some view it as a mere matter of accommodation to mankind, by which God is rendered less strict than he was under the law ; so that they may be fashionable or worldly, and the gospel will come in and make up the deficiencies and save them. The other class view the gospel as a provision of divine benevolence, having for its main design to destroy sin and promote holiness ; and that therefore so far from making it proper for them to be less holy than they ought to be under the law, its whole value consists in its power to make them holy.

2. We see why some people are so much more anxious to convert sinners, than to see the church sanctified and God glorified by the good works of his people.

Many feel a natural sympathy for sinners, and wish to have them saved from hell ; and if that is gained, they have no farther concern. But true saints are most affected by sin as dishonoring God. And they are most distressed to see Christians sin, because it dishonors God more. Some people seem to care but little how the church live, if they can only see the work of conversion go forward. They are not anxious to have God honored. It shows that they are not actuated by the love of holiness, but by a mere compassion for sinners.

3

JUSTIFICATION BY FAITH

Knowing that a man is not justified by the works of the law, but by the faith of Jesus Christ, even we have believed in Jesus Christ, that we might be justified by the faith of Christ, and not by the works of the law ; for by the works of the law shall no flesh be justified.—Gal ii. 16

THIS last sentiment is expressed in the same terms, in the third chapter of Romans. The subject of the present lecture, as I announced last week, is Justification by Faith. The order which I propose to pursue in the discussion is this :

I. Show what justification by law, or legal justification is.

II. Show that by the deeds of the law no flesh can be justified.

III. Show what gospel justification is.

IV. Show what is the effect of gospel justification, or the state into which it brings a person that is justified.

V. Show that gospel justification is by faith.

VI. Answer some inquiries which arise in many minds on this subject.

I. I am to show what legal justification is.

1. In its general legal sense it means not guilty. To justify an individual in this sense, is to declare that he is not guilty of any breach of the law. It is affirming that he has committed no crime. It is pronouncing him innocent.

2. More technically, it is a form of pleading to a charge of crime, where the individual who is charged admits the fact, but brings forward an excuse, on which he claims that he had a right to do as he did, or that he is not blame-

worthy. Thus, if a person is charged with murder, the plea of justification admits that he killed the man, but alleges either that it was done in self-defence and he had a right to kill him, or that it was by unavoidable accident, and he could not help it. In either case, the plea of justification admits the fact, but denies the guilt, on the ground of a sufficient excuse.

II. I am to show that by the deeds of the law there shall no flesh be justified. And this is true under either form of justification.

1. Under the first, or general form of justification. In this case, the burden of proof is on the accuser, who is held to prove the facts charged. And in this case, he only needs to prove that a crime has been committed once. If it is proved once, the individual is guilty. He cannot be justified, in this way, by the law. He is found guilty. It is not available for him to urge that he has done more good than hurt, or that he has kept God's law longer than he has broken it, but he must make it out that he has fulfilled every jot and tittle of the law. Who can be justified by the law in this way ? No one.

2. Nor under the second, or technical form of justification. In this case, the burden of proof lies on him who makes the plea. When he pleads in justification he admits the fact alleged, and therefore he must make good his excuse, or fail. There are two points to be regarded. The thing pleaded as an excuse must be *true*, and it must be a good and sufficient excuse or justification, not a frivolous apology, or one that does not meet the case. If it is not true, or if it is insufficient, and especially if it reflects on the court or government, it is an infamous aggravation of his offence. You will see the bearing of this remark, by and by.

I will now mention some of the prominent reasons which sinners are in the habit of pleading as a justification, and will show what is the true nature and bearing of these excuses, and the light in which they stand before God. I have not time to name all these pleas, but will only refer to two of each of the classes I have described, those which are good if true, and those which are true but unavailing.

(1.) Sinners often plead their sinful nature, as a justification.

This excuse is a good one, if it is true. If it is true, as they pretend, that God has given them a nature which is itself sinful, and the necessary actings of their nature are sin, it is a good excuse for sin, and in the face of heaven and earth, and at the day of judgment, will be a good plea in justification. God must annihilate the reason of all the rational universe, before they will ever blame you for sin if God made you sin, or if he gave you a nature that is itself sinful. How can your nature be sinful ? What is sin ? Sin is a transgression of the law. There is no other sin but this. Now, does the law say you must not have such a nature as you have ? Nothing like it.

The fact is, this doctrine overlooks the distinction between sin and the occasion of sin. The bodily appetites and constitutional susceptibilities of body and mind, when strongly excited, become the occasion of sin. So it was with Adam. No one will say that Adam had a sinful nature. But he had, by his constitution, an appetite for food and a desire for knowledge. These were not sinful, but were as God made them, and were necessary to fit him to live in this world as a subject of God's moral government ; but being strongly excited, as you know, led to prohibited indulgence, and thus became the occasions of his sinning against God. They were innocent in themselves, but he yielded to them in a sinful manner, and that was his sin. When the sinner talks about his sinful nature as a justification, he confounds these innocent appetites and susceptibilities, with sin itself. By so doing, he in fact, charges God foolishly, and accuses him of giving him a sinful nature, when in fact his nature, in all its elements, is essential to moral agency, and God has made it as well as it could be made, and perfectly adapted to the circumstances in which he lives in this world. The truth is. man's nature is all right, and is as well fitted to love and obey God as to hate and disobey him. Sinner ! the day is not far distant, when it will be known whether this is a good excuse or not. Then you will see whether you can face your Maker down in this way ; and when he charges you with sin, turn round and throw the blame back upon him.

Do you inquire what influence Adam's sin has then had in producing the sin of his posterity ? I answer, it has subjected them to aggravated temptation, but has by no means rendered their nature in itself sinful.

2. Another excuse coming under the same class, is inability. This also is a good excuse if it is true. If sinners are really unable to obey God, this is a good plea in justification. When you are charged with sin, in not obeying the laws of God, you have only to show, if you can, by good proof, that God has required what you were not able to perform, and the whole intelligent universe will resound with the verdict of "not guilty." If you have not natural power to obey God, they must give this verdict, or cease to be reasonable beings. For it is a first law of reason, that no being has a right to do what he has no power to do.

Suppose God should require you to undo something which you have done. This, every one will see, is a natural impossibility. Now, are you to blame for not doing it ? God requires repentance of past sins, and not that you should undo them. Now, suppose it was your duty, on the first of January, to warn a certain individual, who is now dead. Are you under obligation to warn that individual ? No. That is an impossibility. All that God

can now require is, that you should repent. It never can
be your duty, now, to warn that sinner. God may hold
you responsible for not doing your duty to him when it was
in your power. But it would be absurd to make it your
duty to do what is not in your power to do.

This plea being false, and throwing the blame of tryanny
on God, is an infamous aggravation of the offence. If God
requires you to do what you have no power to do, it is
tyranny. And what God requires is on penalty of eternal
death—he threatens an infinite penalty for not doing what
you have no power to do, and so he is an infinite tyrant.
This plea, then, charges God with infinite tyranny, and is
not only insufficient for the sinner's justification, but is a
horrible aggravation of his offence.

Let us vary the case a little. Suppose God requires
you to repent for not doing what you never had natural
ability to do. You must either repent, then, of not doing
what you had no natural power to do, or you must go to
hell. Now, you can neither repent of this, nor can he
make you repent of it. What is repentance ? It is to
blame yourself and justify God. But if you had no power,
you can do neither. It is a natural impossibility that a
rational being should ever blame himself for not doing what
he is conscious he had not power to do. Nor can you justify
God. Until the laws of mind are reversed, the verdict of
all intelligent beings must pronounce it infinite tyranny to
require that which there is no power to perform.

Suppose God should call you to account, and require
you to repent for not flying. By what process can he
make you blame yourself for not flying, when you are conscious that you have no wings, and no power to fly ? If
he could cheat you into the belief that you had the power,
and make you believe a lie, then you might repent. But
what sort of a way is that for God to take with his creatures ?

What do you mean, sinner, by bringing such an excuse ? Do you mean to have it go, that you have never sinned ? It is a strange contradiction you make, when you admit that you ought to repent, and in the next breath say you have no power to repent. You ought to take your ground, one way or the other. If you mean to rely on this excuse, come out with it in full, and take your ground before God's bar, and say, " Lord I am not going to repent at all—I am not under any obligation to repent, for I have not power to obey thy law, and therefore I plead not guilty absolutely, for I have never sinned ! "

In which of these ways can any one of you be justified? Will you, dare you, take ground on this excuse, and throw back the blame upon God ?

3. Another excuse which sinners offer for their continued impenitence is their wicked heart.

This excuse is true, but it is not sufficient. The first two that I mentioned, you recollect, were good if they had been true, but they were false. This is true, but is no excuse. What is a wicked heart ? It is not the bodily organ which we call the heart, but the affection of the soul, the wicked disposition, the wicked feelings, the actings of the mind. If these will justify you, they will justify the devil himself. Has he not as wicked a heart as you have ? Suppose you had committed murder, and you should be put on trial and plead this plea. " It is true," you would say, " I killed the man but then I have such a thirst for blood, and such a hatred of mankind, that I cannot help committing murder, whenever I have an opportunity." " Horrible ! " the judge would exclaim, " Horrible ! Let the gallows be set up immediately, and let this fellow be hung before I leave the bench ; such a wretch ought not to live an hour. Such a plea ! Why, that is the very reason he ought to be hung, if he has such a thirst for blood, that no man is safe." Such is the sinner's plea of a wicked heart in justification of sin.   "Out of thine own mouth will I condemn thee, thou wicked servant."

4. Another great excuse which people make is, the conduct of Christians.

Ask many a man among your neighbors why he is not religious, and he will point you at once to the conduct of Christians as his excuse.   "These Christians," he will say, "are no better than anybody else ; when I see them live as they profess, I shall think it time for me to attend to religion."   Thus he is hiding behind the sins of Christians. He shows that he knows how Christians ought to live, and therefore he cannot plead that he has sinned through ignorance.   But what does it amount to as a ground of justification ?   I admit the fact that Christians behave very badly, and do much that is entirely contrary to their profession.   But is that a good excuse for you ?   So far from it, this is itself one of the strongest reasons why you ought to be religious.   You know so well how Christians ought to live, you are bound to show an example.   If you had followed them ignorantly because you did not know any better, and had fallen into sin in that way, it would be a different case.   But the plea, as it stands, shows that you knew they are wrong, which is the very reason why you ought to be right, and exert a better influence than they do.   Instead of following them, and doing wrong because they do, you ought to break off from them, and rebuke them, and pray for them, and try to lead them in a better way.   This excuse, then, is true in fact, but unavailing in justification.   You only make it an excuse for charging God foolishly. and instead of clearing you, it only adds to your dreadful, damning guilt.   A fine plea this, to get behind some deacon, or some elder in the church, and there shoot your arrows of malice and cavilling at God !

Who among you, then, can be justified by the law ? Who has kept it ?   Who has got a good excuse for breaking it ? Who dare go to the bar of God on these pleas, and face his Maker with such apologies ?

III. I am to show what gospel justification is.

First—Negatively.

1. Gospel justification is not the imputed righteousness of Jesus Christ.

Under the gospel, sinners are not justified by having the obedience of Jesus Christ set down to their account, as if he had obeyed the law for them, or in their stead. It is not an uncommon mistake to suppose, that when sinners are justified under the gospel, they are accounted righteous in the eye of the law, by having the obedience or righteousness of Christ imputed to them. I have not time to enter into an examination of this subject now. I can only say this idea is absurd and impossible, for this reason, that Jesus Christ was bound to obey the law for himself, and could no more perform works of supererogation, or obey on our account, than anybody else. Was it not his duty to love the Lord his God, with all his heart, and soul, and mind, and strength, and to love his neighbor as himself ? Certainly ; and if he had not done so, it would have been sin. The only work of supererogation he could perform was to submit to sufferings that were not deserved. This is called his obedience unto death, and this is set down to our account. But if his obedience of the law is set down to our account, why are we called on to repent and obey the law ourselves ? Does God exact double service, yes, triple service—first to have the law obeyed by the surety for us, then that he must suffer the penalty for us, and then that we must repent and obey ourselves ? No such thing is demanded. It is not required that the obedience of another should be imputed to us. All we owe is perpetual obedience to the law of benevolence. And for this there can be no substitute. If we fail of this, we must endure the penalty, or receive a free pardon.

2. Justification by faith does not mean that faith is accepted as a substitute for personal holiness, or that by an arbitrary constitution, faith is imputed to us instead of personal obedience to the law.

Some suppose that justification is this, that the necessity of personal holiness is set aside, and that God arbitrarily dispenses with the requirement of the law, and imputes faith as a substitute. But this is not the way. Faith is accounted for just what it is, and not something else that it is not. Abraham's faith was imputed unto him for righteousness, because it was itself an act of righteousness, and because it worked by love, and thus produced holiness. Justifying faith is holiness, so far as it goes, and produces holiness of heart and life, and is imputed to the believer as holiness, not instead of holiness.

Nor does justification by faith imply that a sinner is justified by faith without good works, or personal holiness.

Some suppose that justification by faith only, is without any regard to good works, or holiness. They have understood this from what Paul has said, where he insists so largely on justification by faith. But it should be borne in mind that Paul was combating the error of the Jews, who expected to be justified by obeying the law. In opposition to this error, Paul insists on it that justification is by faith, without works of law. He does not mean that good works are unnecessary to justification, but that works of law are not good works, because they spring from legal considerations, from hope and fear, and not from faith that works by love. But inasmuch as a false theory had crept into the church on the other side, James took up the matter, and showed them that they had misunderstood Paul. And to show this, he takes the case of Abraham our father justified by works when he had offered Isaac his son upon the altar? Seest thou how faith wrought with his works, and by works was faith made perfect? And the scripture was fulfilled, which saith, Abraham believed **God,** and it was imputed unto him for righteousness : and he was called the Friend of God. Ye see then how that by works a man is justified, and not by faith only." This epistle was supposed to contradict Paul, and some of the ancient churches rejected it on that account. But they overlooked the fact that Paul was speaking of one kind of works, and James of another. Paul was speaking of works performed from legal motives. But he has everywhere insisted on good works springing from faith, or the righteousness of faith, as indispensable to salvation. All that he denies is that works of law, or works grounded on legal motives, have anything to do in the matter of justification. And James teaches the same thing, when he teaches that men are justified, not by works nor by faith alone, but by faith together with the works of faith : or as Paul expresses it, faith that works by love. You will bear in mind that I am speaking of gospel justification, which is very different from legal justification.

Secondly—Positively.

4. Gospel justification, or justification by faith, consists in pardon and acceptance with God.

When we say that men are justified by faith and holiness, we do not mean that they are accepted on the ground of law, but that they are treated as if they were righteous, on account of their faith and works of faith. This is the method which God takes, in justifying a sinner. Not that faith is the foundation of justification. The foundation is in Christ. But this is the manner in which sinners are pardoned, and accepted, and justified, that if they repent, believe, and become holy, their past sins shall be forgiven, for the sake of Christ.

Here it will be seen how justification under the gospel differs from justification under the law. Legal justification is a declaration of actual innocence and freedom from

blame. Gospel justification is pardon and acceptance, as
if he was righteous, but on other grounds than his own
obedience. When the apostle says, " By deeds of law shall
no flesh be justified, he uses justification as a lawyer, in a
strictly legal sense. But when he speaks of justification
by faith, he speaks not of legal justification, but of a person's being treated as if he were righteous.

IV. I will now proceed to show the effect of this method
of justification ; or the state into which it brings those who
are justified.

1. The first item to be observed is, that when an individual is pardoned, the penalty of the law is released.
The first effect of a pardon is to arrest and set aside the
execution of the penalty. It admits that the penalty was
deserved, but sets it aside. Then, so far as punishment is
concerned, the individual has no more to fear from the law,
than if he had never transgressed. He is entirely released.
Those, then, who are justified by true faith, as soon as they
are pardoned, need no more be influenced by fear or punishment. The penalty is as effectually set aside, as if it
had never been incurred.

2. The next effect of pardon is, to remove all the lia-
bilities incurred in consequence of transgression, such as
forfeiture of goods, or incapacity for being a witness, or
holding any office under goverment. A real pardon re-
moves all these, and restores the individual back to where
he was before he transgressed. So, under the government
of God, the pardoned sinner is restored to the favor of
God. He is brought back into a new relation, and stands
before God and is treated by him, so far as the law is concerned, as if he were innocent. It does not suppose or declare him to be really innocent, but the pardon restores
him to the same state as if he were.

3. Another operation of pardon under God's government is, that the individual is restored to sonship. In

other words, it brings him into such a relation to God, that
he is received and treated as really a child of God.

Suppose the son of a sovereign on the throne had committed murder, and was convicted and condemned to die.
A pardon, then, would not only deliver him from death,
but restore him to his place in the family. God's children
have all gone astray, and entered into the service of the
devil; but the moment a pardon issues to them, they are
brought back ; they receive a spirit of adoption, are sealed
heirs of God, and restored to all the privileges of children
of God.

4. Another thing effected by justification is to secure
all needed grace to rescue themselves fully out of the snare
of the devil, and all the innumerable entanglements in
which they are involved by sin.

Beloved, if God were merely to pardon you, and then
leave you to get out of sin as you could by yourselves, of
what use would your pardon be to you ? None in the
world. If a child runs away from his father's house, and
wanders in a forest, and falls into a deep pit, and the father
finds him and undertakes to save him ; if he merely pardons him for running away, it will be of no use unless he
lifts him up from the pit, and leads him out of the forest.
So in the scheme of redemption, whatever helps and aids
you need, are all guaranteed, if you believe. If God undertakes to save you, he pledges all the light and grace and
help that are necessary to break the chains of Satan and
the entanglements of sin, and leads you back to your
Father's house.

I know when individuals are first broken down under a
sense of sin, and their hearts gush out with tenderness,
they look over their past lives and feel condemned and see
that it is all wrong, and then they break down at God's
feet and give themselves away to Jesus Christ ; they rejoice
greatly in the idea that they have done with sin. But in

a little time they begin to feel the pressure of old habits and former influences, and they see so much to be done before they overcome them all, that they often get discouraged and cry, "O, what shall I do, with so many enemies to meet, and so little strength of resolution or firmness of purpose to overcome them?" Let me tell you, beloved, that if God has undertaken to save you, you have only to keep near to him, and he will carry you through. You need not fear your enemies. Though the heavens should thunder and the earth rock, and the elements melt, you need not tremble, nor fear for enemies without or enemies within. God is for you, and who can be against you? "Who is he that condemneth? It is Christ that died, yea, rather that is risen again, who is even at the right hand of God, who also maketh intercession for us."

5. Justification enlists all the divine attributes in your favor, as much as if you had never sinned.

See that holy angel, sent on an errand of love to some distant part of the universe. God's eye follows him, and if he sees him likely to be injured in any way, all the divine attributes are enlisted at once to protect and sustain him. Just as absolutely are they all pledged for you, if you are justified, to protect, and support, and save you. Notwithstanding you are not free from remaining sin, and are so totally unworthy of God's love, yet if you are truly justified, the only wise and eternal God is pledged for your salvation. And shall you tremble and be faint-hearted with such support?

If a human goverment pardons a criminal, it is then pledged to protect him as a subject, as much as if he had never committed a crime. So it is when God justifies a sinner. The Apostle says, "Being justified by faith, we have peace with God." Henceforth, God is on his side, and pledged as his faithful and eternal Friend.

Gospel justification differs from legal justification, in this respect : If the law justifies an individual, it holds no longer than he remains innocent. As soon as he transgresses once, his former justification is of no more avail. But when the gospel justifies a sinner, it is not so ; but " if any man sin, we have an Advocate with the Father, Jesus Christ the righteous." A new relation is now constituted, entirely peculiar. The sinner is now brought out from under the covenant of works, and placed under the covenant of grace. He no longer retains God's favor by the tenure of absolute and sinless obedience. If he sins, now, he is not thrust back again under the law, but receives the benefit of the new covenant. If he is justified by faith, and so made a child of God, he receives the treatment of a child, and is corrected, and chastised, and humbled, and brought back again. "The gifts and callings of God are without repentance." The meaning of that is not, that God calls and saves the sinner without his repenting, but that God never changes his mind when once he undertakes the salvation of a soul.

I know this is thought by some to be very dangerous doctrine, to teach that believers are perpetually justified— because, say they, it will embolden men to sin. Indeed ! To tell a man that has truly repented of sin, and heartily renounced sin, and sincerely desires to be free from sin, that God will help him and certainly give him the victory over sin, will embolden him to commit sin ! Strange logic that ! If this doctrine emboldens any man to commit sin, it only shows that he never did repent ; that he never hated sin, and never loved God for his own sake, but only feigned repentance, and if he loved God it was only a selfish love, because he thought God was going to do him a favor. If he truly hated sin, the consideration that notwithstanding all his unworthiness, God had received him as a child, and would give him a child's treatment, is the very thing to

break him down and melt his heart in the most godly sor-
sow. O, how often has the child of God, melted in adoring wonder at the goodness of God in using means to
bring him back, instead of sending him to hell, as he deserved ! What consideration is calculated to bring him
lower in the dust, than the thought that notwithstanding
all God had done for him, and the gracious help God was
always ready to afford him, he should wander away again,
when his name was written in the Lamb's book of life !

6. It secures the discipline of the covenant. God has
pledged himself that if any who belong to Christ go astray,
he will use the discipline of the covenant, and bring them
back. In the eighty-ninth psalm, God says, putting David
for Christ, " If his children forsake my law, and walk not
in my judgments : if they break my statutes, and keep not
my commandments ; then will I visit their transgression
with the rod, and their iniquity with stripes. Neverthe-
less my loving kindness will I not utterly take from him,
nor suffer my faithfulness to fail. My covenant will I not
break, nor alter the thing that is gone out of my lips."

Thus you see that professors of religion may always
expect to be more readily visited with God's judgments, if
they get out of the way, than the impenitent. The sinner
may grow fat, and live in riches, and have no bands in his
death, all according to God's established principles of government. But let a child of God forsake his God, and go
after riches or any other worldly object, and as certain as
he is a child, God will smite him with his rod. And when
he is smitten and brought back, he will say with the Psalm-
ist ," It is good for me that I have been afflicted, that I
might learn thy statutes. Before I was afflicted, I went
astray, but now have I kept thy word." Perhaps some of
you have known what it is to be afflicted in this way, and to
feel that it was good.

7. Another effect of gospel justification is, to insure

sanctification. It not only insures all the means of sanctification, but the actual accomplishment of the work, so that the individual who is truly converted, will surely persevere in obedience till he is fitted for heaven and actually saved.

V. I am to show that this is justification by faith.

Faith is the medium by which the blessing is conveyed to the believer. The proof of this is in the Bible. The text declares it expressly. "Knowing that a man is not justified by the works of the law, but by the faith of Jesus Christ, even we have believed in Jesus Christ, that we might be justified by the faith of Christ, and not by the works of the law : for by the works of the law shall no flesh be justified." The subject is too often treated of in the New Testament to be necessary to go into a labored proof. It is manifest, from the necessity of the case, that if men are saved at all, they must be justified in this way, and not by works of law, for "by the deeds of the law shall no flesh be justified."

VI. I will now answer several inquiries which may naturally arise in your minds, growing out of this subject.

1. "Why is justification said to be by faith, rather than by repentance, or love, or any other grace."

Answer. It is no where said that men are justified or saved *for* faith, as the ground of their pardon, but only that they are justified *by* faith, as the medium or instrument. If it is asked why faith is appointed as the instrument, rather than any other exercise of the mind, the answer is, because of the nature and effect of faith. No other exercise could be appointed. What is faith ? It is that confidence in God which leads us to love and obey him. We are therefore justified by faith *because* we are sanctified by faith. Faith is the appointed instrument of our justification, because it is the natural instrument of sanctification. It is the instrument of bringing us back to obedience, and therefore is designated as the means of obtaining the blessings of that return. It is not imputed to us, by an arbitrary act, *for* what it is not, but for what it is, as the foundation of all real obedience to God. This is the reason why faith is made the medium through which pardon comes. It is simply set down to us for what it really is ; because it first leads us to obey God, from a principle of love to God. We are forgiven our sins on account of Christ. It is our duty to repent and obey God, and when we do so, this is imputed to us as what it is, holiness, or obedience to God. But for the forgiveness of our past sins, we must rely on Christ. And therefore justification is said to be by faith in Jesus Christ.

2. The second query is of great importance :—" What is justifying faith ? What must I believe, in order to be saved ? "

Answer. (1) Negatively, justifying faith does not consist in believing that your sins are forgiven. If that were necessary, you would have to believe it before it was done, or to believe a lie. Remember your sins are not forgiven *until* you believe. But if saving faith is believing that they are already forgiven, it is believing a thing before it takes place, which is absurd. You cannot believe your sins are forgiven, before you have the evidence that they are forgiven ; and you cannot have the evidence that they are forgiven until it is true that they are forgiven, and they cannot be forgiven until you exercise saving faith. Therefore saving faith must be believing something else.

Nor (2) does saving faith consist in believing that you shall be saved at all. You have no right to believe that you shall be saved at all, until after you have exercised justifying or saving faith.

But (3) justifying faith consists in believing the atonement of Christ, or believing the record which God has given of his Son.

The correctness of this definition has been doubted by some; and I confess my own mind has undergone a change on this point. It is said that Abraham believed God, and it was imputed to him for righteousness. But what did Abraham believe? He believed that he should have a son. Was this all? By no means. But his faith included the great blessing that depended on that event, that the Messiah, the Saviour of the world, should spring from him. This was the great subject of the Abrahamic covenant, and it depended on his having a son. Of course, Abraham's faith included the "Desire of all Nations," and was faith in Christ. The apostle Paul has showed this, at full length, in the third chapter of Galatians, that the sum of the covenant was, "In thee shall all nations be blessed." In verse 16, he says, "Now to Abraham and his seed were the promises made. He saith not, And to seeds, as of many; but as of one: And to thy seed, which is Christ."

It is said that in the 11th of Hebrews, the saints are not all spoken of as having believed in Christ. But if you examine carefully, you will find that in all cases, faith in Christ is either included in what they believe, or fairly implied by it. Take the case of Abel. "By faith Abel offered unto God a more excellent sacrifice than Cain, by which he obtained witness that he was righteous, God testifying of his gifts: and by it he being dead yet speaketh." Why was his sacrifice more excellent? Because, by offering the firstlings of his flock, he recognized the necessity of the atonement, and that "without the shedding of blood there is no remission." Cain was a proud infidel, and offered the fruits of the ground, as a mere thank offering, for the blessings of Providence, without any admission that he was a sinner, and needed an atonement, as the ground on which he could hope for pardon.

Some suppose that an individual might exercise justifying faith while denying the divinity and atonement of

Jesus Christ. I deny this. The whole sum and substance of revelation, like converging rays, all centre on Jesus Christ, his divinity and atonement. All that the prophets and other writers of the Old Testament say about salvation comes to him. The Old Testament and the New, all the types and shadows, point to him. All the Old Testament saints were saved by faith in him. Their faith terminated in the coming Messiah, as that of the New Testament saints did in the Messiah already come. In the 15th chapter of 1st Corinthians, the apostle Paul shows what place he would assign to this doctrine: "For I delivered unto you first of all that which I also received, how that Christ died for our sins according to the scriptures ; and that he was buried, and that he rose again the third day according to the scriptures." Mark that expression, "first of all." It proves that Paul preached that Christ died for sinners, as the "first," or primary doctrine of the gospel. And so you will find it, from one end of the Bible to the other, that the attention of men was directed to this new and living way, as the only way of salvation. This truth is the only truth that can sanctify men. They may believe a thousand other things, but this is the great source of sanctification, "God in Christ, reconciling the world unto himself." And this alone can therefore be justifying faith.

There may be many other acts of faith, that may be right and acceptable to God. But nothing is justifying faith but believing the record that God has given of his Son. Simply believing what God has revealed on any point, is an act of faith ; but justifying faith fastens on Christ, takes hold of his atonement, and embraces him as the only ground of pardon and salvation. There may be faith in prayer, the faith that is in exercise in offering up prevailing prayer to God. But that is not properly justifying faith.

3. " When are men justified ? "

This is also an enquiry often made.   I answer—Just as soon as they believe in Christ, with the faith which worketh by love.   Sinner, you need not go home from this meeting under the wrath of Almighty God.   You may be justified here, on the spot, now, if you will only believe in Christ.   Your pardon is ready, made out and sealed with the broad seal of heaven ; and the blank will be filled up, and the gracious pardon delivered, as soon as by one act of faith, you receive Jesus Christ as he is offered in the gospel.

4. " How can I know whether I am in a state of justification or not ? "

Answer.   You can know it in no way, except by inference.   God has not revealed it in the Scriptures, that you, or any other individuals, are justified ; but he has set down the characteristics of a justified person, and declared that all who have these characteristics are justified.

(1.) Have you the witness of the Spirit ?   All who are justified have this.   They have intercourse with the Holy Ghost, he explains the Scriptures to them, and leads them to see their meaning, he leads them to the Son and to the Father ; and reveals the Son in them, and reveals the Father.   Heve you this ?   If you have, you are justified. If not, you are yet in your sins.

(2.) Have you the fruits of the Spirit ?   They are love, joy, peace, and so on.   These are matters of human consciousness ; have you them ?   If so, you are justified.

(3.) Have you peace with God ?   The apostle says, " Being justified by faith, we have peace with God." Christ says to his disciples, " My peace I give unto you ; not as the world giveth give I unto you."   And again, " Come unto me, all ye that labor and are heavy laden, and I will give you rest."   Do you find *rest* in Christ ?   Is your peace like a river, flowing gently through your soul, and filling you with calm and heavenly delight? **Or do** you feel a sense of condemnation before God ?

Do you feel a sense of acceptance with God, of pardoned sin, of communion with God ? This must be a matter of experience, if it exists. Don't imagine you *can be in* a justified state, and yet have no evidence of it. You may have great peace in reality, filling your soul, and yet not draw the inference that you are justified. I remember the time, when my mind was in a state of such sweet peace, that it seemed to me as if all nature was listening for God to speak ; but yet I was not aware that this was the peace of God, or that it was evidence of my being in a justified state. I thought I had lost all my conviction, and actually undertook to bring back the sense of condemnation that I had before. I did not draw the inference that I was justified, till after the love of God was so shed abroad in my soul by the Holy Ghost, that I was compelled to cry out, "Lord, it is enough, I can bear no more." I do not believe it possible for the sense of condemnation to remain, where the act of pardon is already past.

4. Have you the spirit of adoption ? If you are justified, you are also adopted, as one of God's dear children, and he has sent forth his Spirit into your heart, so that you naturally cry, "Abba, Father !" He seems to you just like a father, and you want to call him father. Do you know any thing of this ? It is one thing to *call* God your father in heaven, and another thing to *feel* towards him as a father. This is one evidence of a justified state, when God gives the spirit of adoption.

CONCLUSION

I. I would go around to all my dear hearers to-night, and ask them one by one, "Are you in a state of justification ? Do you honestly think you are justified ?"

I have briefly run over the subject, and showed what

justification is not, and what it is, how you can be saved, and the evidences of justification. Have you it? Would you dare to die now? Suppose the loud thunders of the last trumpet were now to shake the universe, and you should see the Son of God coming to judgment—are you ready? Could you look up calmly and say, "Father, this is a solemn sight, but Christ has died, and God has justified me, and who is he that shall condemn me?"

II. If you think you ever was justified, and yet have not at present the evidence of it, I want to make an inquiry. Are you under the discipline of the covenant?—If not, have you any reason to believe you ever were justified? God's covenant with you, if you belong to Christ, is this—"If they backslide, I will visit their iniquity with the rod, and chasten them with stripes." Do you feel the stripes? Is God awakening your mind, and convicting your conscience, is he smiting you? If not, where are the evidences that he is dealing with you as a son? If you are not walking with God, and at the same time are not under chastisement, you cannot have any good reason to believe you are God's children.

III. Those of you who have evidence that you are justified, should maintain your relation to God, and live up to your real privileges. This is immensely important. There is no virtue in being distrustful and unbelieving. It is important to your growth in grace. One reason why many Christians do not grow in grace is, that they are afraid to claim the privileges of God's children which belong to them. Rely upon it, beloved, this is no virtuous humility, but criminal unbelief. If you have the evidence that you are justified, take the occasion from it to press forward to holiness of heart, and come to God with all the boldness that an angel would, and know how near you are to him. It is your duty to do so. Why should you hold back? Why are you afraid to recognize the covenant of grace, in its full extent ?   Here are the provisions of your Father's house, all ready and free ; and are you converted and justified, and restored to his favor, and yet afraid to sit down at your Father's table ?   Do not plead that you are so unworthy.   This is nothing but self-righteousness and unbelief.   True, you are so unworthy.   But if you are justified, that is no longer a bar.   It is now your duty to take hold of the promises as belonging to you.   Take any promise you can find in the Bible, that is applicable, and go with it to your Father, and plead it before him, believing.   Do you think he will deny it ?   These exceeding great and precious promises were given you for this very purpose, that you may become a partaker of the divine nature.   Why then should you doubt ?   Come along, beloved, come along up to the privileges that belong to you, and take hold of the love, and peace, and joy, offered to you in this holy gospel.

IV. If you are not in a state of justification, however much you have done, and prayed, and suffered, you are nothing.   If you have not believed in Christ, if you have not received and trusted in him, as he is set forth in the gospel, you are yet in a state of condemnation and wrath. You may have been, for weeks and months, and even for years, groaning with distress, but for all that, you are still in the gall of bitterness.   Here you see the line drawn ; the moment you pass this, you are in a state of justification.

Dear hearer, are you now in a state of wrath ?   Now believe in Christ.   All your waiting and groaning will not bring you any nearer.   Do you say you want more conviction ?   I tell you to come now to Christ.   Do you say you must wait till you have prayed more ?   What is the use of praying in unbelief ?   Will the prayers of a condemned rebel avail ?   Do you say you are so unworthy ? But Christ died for such as you.   He comes right to you

now, on your seat. Where do you sit ? Where is that in
dividual I am speaking to ? Sinner, you need not wait.
You need not go home in your sins, with that heavy load
on your heart. Now is the day of salvation. Hear the
word of God. "If thou believe in thine heart in the Lord
Jesus Christ, and if thou confess with thy mouth that God
raised him from the dead, thou shalt be saved."

Do you say, "What must I believe ?" Believe just
what God says of his Son ; believe any of those great fundamental truths which God has revealed respecting the way
of salvation, and rest your soul on it, and you shall be
saved. Will you now trust Jesus Christ to dispose of you ?
Have you confidence enough in Christ to leave yourself with
him, to dispose of your body and your soul, for time and
eternity ? Can you say

> " Here, Lord, I give myself away ;
> 'Tis all that I can do ? "

Perhaps you are trying to pray yourself out of your
difficulties before coming to Christ. Sinner, it will do no
good. Now, cast yourself down at his feet, and leave your
soul in his hands. Say to him, " Lord, I give myself to
thee, with all my powers of body and of mind ; use me and
dispose of me as thou wilt, for thine own glory ; I know
thou wilt do right, and that is all I desire." Will you do
it ?

4

THE WAY OF SALVATION

Sirs, what must I do to be saved ? And they said, Believe on the Lord Jesus Christ. Who of God is made unto us wisdom, and righteousness, and santi cation, and redemption.—Acts xvi. 30, 31, with 1 Cor. i. 30

THERE can be no objection to putting these texts together in this manner as only a clause in the first of them is omitted, which is not essential to the sense, and which is irrelevant to my present purpose.

In the passage first quoted, the apostle tells the inquiring jailer, who wished to know what he must do to be saved, "Believe on the Lord Jesus Christ and thou shalt be saved." And in the other he adds the explanatory remark, telling what a Saviour Jesus Christ is, "Who of God is made unto us wisdom, and righteousness, and sanctification, and redemption." The following is the order in which I design to discuss the subject to-night :

I. Show what salvation is.

II. Show the way of salvation.

1. What is salvation ?

Salvation includes several things—sanctification, justification, and eternal life and glory. The two prime ideas, are sanctification and justification. Sanctification is the purifying of the mind, or making it holy. Justification relates to the manner in which we are accepted and treated by God.

II. The way of salvation.

1. It is by faith, in opposition to works.

Here I design to take a brief view of the gospel plan of salvation, and exhibit it especially in contrast with the original plan on which it was proposed to save mankind.

76

Originally, the human race was put on the foundation of law for salvation ; so that, if saved at all, they were to be saved on the ground of perfect and eternal obedience to the law of God. Adam was the natural head of the race. It has been supposed by many, that there was a covenant made with Adam such as this, that if he continued to obey the law for a limited period all his posterity should be confirmed in holiness and happiness forever. What the reason is for this belief, I am unable to ascertain ; I am not aware that the doctrine is taught in the Bible. And if it is true, the condition of mankind now does not differ materially from what it was at first. If the salvation of the race originally turned wholly on the obedience of one man, I do not see how it could be called a covenant of works so far as the race is concerned. For if their weal or woe was suspended on the conduct of one head, it was a covenant of grace to them, in the same manner that the present system is a covenant of grace. For according to that view, all that related to works depended on one man, just as it does under the gospel ; and the rest of the race had no more to do with works, than they have now, but all that related to works was done by the representative. Now, I have supposed, and there is nothing in the Bible to the contrary, that if Adam had continued in obedience forever, his posterity would have stood forever on the same ground, and must have obeyed the law themselves forever in order to be saved. It may have been, that if he had obeyed always, the natural influence of his example would have brought about such a state of things, that as a matter of fact all his posterity would have continued in holiness. But the salvation of each individual would still have depended on his own works. But if the works of the first father were to be so set to the account of the race, that on account of his obedience they were to be secured in holiness and happiness forever, I do not see wherein it differs materially from the covenant of grace, or the gospel.

As a matter of fact, Adam was the natural head of the human race, and his sin has involved them in its consequences, but not on the principle that his sin is literally accounted their sin. The truth is simply this ; that from the relation in which he stood as their natural head, as a matter of fact his sin has resulted in the sin and ruin of his posterity, I suppose that mankind were originally all under a covenant of works, and that Adam was not so their head or representative, that his obedience or disobedience involved them irresistibly in sin and condemnation, irrespective of their own acts. As a fact it resulted so, that " by one man's disobedience many were made sinners ; " as the apostle tells us in the 5th of Romans. So that, when Adam had fallen, there was not the least hope, by the law, of saving any of mankind. Then was revealed *the plan,* which had been provided in the counsels of eternity, on foresight of this event, for saving mankind by a proceeding of mere grace. Salvation was now placed on an entire new foundation, by a Covenant of Redemption. You will find this covenant in the 89th Psalm, and other places in the Old Testament. This, you will observe, is a covenant between the Father and the Son, regarding the salvation of mankind, and is the foundation of another covenant, the covenant of grace. In the covenant of redemption, man is no party at all, but merely the subject of the covenant ; the parties being God the Father and the Son. In this covenant, the Son is made the head or representative of his people. Adam was the natural head of the human family, and Christ is the covenant head of his church.

On this covenant of redemption was founded the covenant of grace. In the covenant of redemption, the Son stipulated with the Father, to work out an atonement ; and the Father stipulated that he should have a seed, or people, gathered out of the human race. The **covenant** of grace was made with men and was revealed to **Adam,** after the fall, and more fully revealed to Abraham. Of this covenant, Jesus Christ was to be the Mediator, or he that should administer it. It was a covenant of grace, in opposition to the original covenant of works, under which Adam and his posterity were placed at the beginning ; and salvation was now to be by faith, instead of works, be· cause the obedience and death of Jesus Christ were to be regarded as the reason why any individual was to be saved, and not each one's personal obedience. Not that his obedience was, strictly speaking, performed for us. As a **man,** he was under the necessity of obeyng. for himself ; because he had not put himself under the law, and if he did not obey it he became personally a transgressor. And **yet** there is a sense in which it may be said that his obedience is reckoned to our account. His obedience has so highly honored the law, and his death has so fully satisfied the demands of public justice, that grace, (not justice,) has reckoned his righteousness to us. If he had obeyed the law strictly for us, and had owed no obedience for himself, but was at liberty to obey only for us, then I cannot see why justice should not have accounted his obedience to us, and we could have obtained salvation on the score of right. instead of asking it on the score of grace or favor. But it is only in this sense accounted ours, that he, being God and man, having voluntarily assumed our nature, and then voluntarily laying down his life to make atonement, casts such a glory on the law of God, that grace is willing to consider obedience· in such a sense ours, as, on his account, to treat us as if we were righteous.

Christ is also the covenant head of those that believe. He is not the natural head, as Adam was, but our covenant relation to him is such, that whatever is given to him is **given to us.** Whatever he is, both in his divine and human nature ; whatever he has done, either as God or man, is given to us by covenant, or promise, and is absolutely ours. I desire you should understand this. The church, as a body, has never yet understood the fulness and richness of this covenant, and that all there is in Christ is made over to us in the covenant of grace.

And here let me say, that we receive this grace by faith. It is not by works, by anything we do, more or less, previous to the exercise of faith, that we become interested in this righteousness. But as soon as we exercise faith, all that Christ has done, all there is of Christ, all that is contained in the covenant of grace, becomes ours by faith. Hence it is, that the inspired writers make so much of faith. Faith is the voluntary compliance on our part, with the condition of the covenant. It is the eye that discerns, the hand that takes hold, the medium by which we possess the blessings of the covenant. By the act of faith, the soul becomes actually possessed of all that is embraced in that act of faith. If there is not enough received to break the bonds of sin and set the soul at once at liberty, it is because the act has not embraced enough of what Christ is, and what he has done.

I have read the verse from Corinthians, for the purpose of remarking on some of the fundamental things contained in this covenant of grace. " Of him are ye in Christ Jesus, who of God is made unto us wisdom, and righteousness, and sanctification, and redemption." When Christ is received and believed on, he is made to us what is meant by these several particulars. But what is meant ? How and in what sense is Christ our wisdom, and righteousness, and sanctification, and redemption ? I will dwell a few moments on each.

This is a very peculiar verse, and my mind has long dwelt on it with great anxiety to know its exact and full meaning. I have prayed over it, as much as over any

passage in the Bible, that I might be enlightened to understand its real import.   I have long been in the habit,
when my mind fastened on any passage that I did not understand, to pray over it till I felt satisfied.   I have never
dared to preach on this verse, because I never felt fully
satisfied that I understood it.   I think I understand it now.
At all events, I am willing to give my opinion on it.   And
if I have any right knowledge respecting its meaning, I am
sure I have received it from the Spirit of God.

1. In what sense is Christ our wisdom ?

He is often called " the Wisdom of God."   And in the
Book of Proverbs he is called Wisdom.   But how is he
made to us wisdom.

One idea contained in it is, that we have absolutely all
the benefits of his wisdom ; and if we exercise the faith we
ought, we are just as certain to be directed by it, and it is
in all respects just as well for us, as if we had the same
wisdom, originally, of our own.   Else it cannot be true
that he is made unto us wisdom.   As he is the infinite
source of wisdom, how can it be said that he is made unto
us wisdom, unless we are partakers of his wisdom, and have
it guaranteed to us ; so that at any time, if we trust in
him, we may have it as certainly, and in any degree we
need, to guide us infallibly, as if we had it originally ourselves ?   That is what we need from the gospel, and what
the gospel must furnish, to be suited to our necessities.
And the man who has not learned this, has not known any
thing as he ought.   If he thinks his own theorizing and
speculating are going to bring him to any right knowledge
on the subject of religion, he knows nothing at all, as yet.
His carnal, earthly heart, can no more study out the reali-
ties of religion so as to get any available knowledge of them
than the heart of a beast.   " What man knoweth the things
of a man, save the spirit of a man which is in him ?   Even
so the things of God knoweth no man, but the Spirit of

God." What can we know, without experience, of the character or Spirit of God ? Do you say, " We can reason about God." What if we do reason ? What can reason do here ? Suppose here was a mind that was all pure in-tellect, and had no other powers, and I should undertake to teach that pure intellect what it was to love. I could lecture on it, and instruct that pure intellect in the words, so that it could reason and philosophize about love, and yet any body can see that it is impossible to put that pure in-tellect in possession of the idea of what love is, unless it not only has power to exercise love, but has actually exer-cised it ! It is just as if I should talk about colors to a man born blind. He hears the word, but what idea can he attach to it, unless he has seen ? It is impossible to get the idea home to his mind, of the difference of colors. The term is a mere word.

Just so it is in religion. One whose mind has not ex-perienced it, may reason upon it. He may demonstrate the perfections of God, as he would demonstrate a propo-sition in Euclid. But that which is the spirit and life of the gospel, can no more be carried to the mind by mere words, without experience, than love to a pure intellect, or colors to a man born blind. You may so far give him the letter, as to crush him down to hell with conviction ; but to give the spiritual meaning of things, without the Spirit of God, is as absurd as to lecture a blind man about colors.

These two things, then, are contained in the idea of wisdom. 1. As Christ is our representative, we are inter-ested in all his wisdom, and all the wisdom he has is exer-cised for us. His infinite wisdom is actually employed for our benefit. And, 2, That his wisdom, just as much as is needed, is guaranteed to be always ready to be im-parted to us, whenever we exercise faith in him for wis-dom. From his infinite fulness, in this respect, we may receive all we need. And if we do not receive from him the wisdom which we need, in any and every case, it is because we do not exercise faith.

2. He is made unto us righteousness. What is the meaning of this ?

Here my mind has long labored to understand the distinction which the apostle intended to make between righteousness and sanctification. Righteousness means holiness, or obedience to law ; and sanctification means the same.

My present view of the distinction aimed at is, that by his being made unto us righteousness, the apostle meant to be understood, that Christ is our *outward* righteousness; or that his obedience is, under the covenant of grace, accounted to us. Not in the sense that on the footing of justice he obeyed " for us," and God accounts us just, because our substitute has obeyed ; but that we are so interested in his obedience, that as a matter of grace, we are treated as if we had ourselves obeyed.

You are aware there is a view of this subject, which is maintained by some, different from this ; that the righteousness of Christ is so imputed to us, that we are considered as having been always holy. It was at one time extensively maintained that righteousness was so imputed to us, that we had a right to demand salvation, on the score of justice. My view of the matter is entirely different. It is, that Christ's righteousness becomes ours by gift. God has so united us to Christ, as on his account to treat us with favor. It is just like a case, where a father had done some signal service to his country, and the government thinks it proper to reward such signal service with signal reward ; and not only is the individual himself rewarded, but all his family receive favors on his account, because they are the children of a father who had greatly benefitted his country. Human governments do this, and

the ground of it is very plain. It is just so in the divine government. Christ's disciples are in such a sense considered one with him, and God is so highly delighted with the signal service he has done the kingdom, from the circumstances under which he became a Saviour, that God accounts his righteousness to them as if it were their own ; or in other words, treats them just as he would treat Christ himself. As the government of the country, under certain circumstances, treats the son of a father who had greatly benefited the country, just as they would treat the father, and bestow on him the same favors. You will bear in mind, that I am now speaking of what I called the outward righteousness ; I mean, the reason out of the individual, why God accepts and saves them that believe in Christ. And this reason includes both the obedience of Christ to the law, and his obedience unto death, or suffering upon the cross to make atonement.

3. In what sense is Christ made unto us sanctification ?

Sanctification is inward purity. And the meaning is, that he is our inward purity. The control which Christ himself exercises over us, his Spirit working in us, to will and to do, his shedding his love abroad in our hearts, so controlling us that we are ourselves, through the faith which is of the operation of God, made actually holy.

I wish you to get the exact idea here. When it is said that Christ is our sanctification, or our holiness, it is meant that he is the author of our holiness. He is not only the procuring cause, by his atonement and intercession, but by his direct intercourse with the soul he himself produces holiness. He is not the remote but the immediate cause of our being sanctified. He works our works in us, not by suspending our own agency, but he so controls our minds, by the influences of his Spirit in us, in a way perfectly consistent with our freedom, as to sanctify us. And this, also, is received by faith. It is by faith that Christ is received and enthroned as *king* in our hearts ; when the mind, from confidence in Christ, just yields itself up to him, to be led by his Spirit, and guided and controlled by his hand. The act of the mind, that thus throws the soul into the hand of Christ for sanctification, is faith. Nothing is wanting, but for the mind to break off from any confidence in itself, and to give itself up to him, to be led and controlled by him, absolutely : just as the child puts out its little hand to its father, to have him lead it anywhere he pleases. If the child is distrustful, or not willing to be led, or if it has confidence in its own wisdom and strength, it will break away and try to run alone. But if all that self-confidence fails, it will cease from its own efforts, and come and give itself up to its father again, to be led entirely at his will. I suppose this is similar to the act of faith, by which an individual gives his mind up to be led and controlled by Christ. He ceases from his own efforts to guide, and control, and sanctify himself ; and just gives himself up, as yielding as air, and leaves himself in the hands of Christ as his sanctification.

4. It is said Christ is made of God unto us redemption. What are we to understand by that ?

Here the apostle plainly refers to the Jewish practice of redeeming estates, or redeeming relatives that had been sold for debt. When an estate had been sold out of the family, or an individual had been deprived of liberty for debt, they could be redeemed, by paying the price of redemption. There are very frequent allusions in the Bible to this practice of redemption. And where Christ is spoken of as our redemption, I suppose it means just what it says. While we are in our sins, under the law, we are sold as slaves, in the hand of public justice, bound over to death, and have no possible way to redeem ourselves from the curse of the law. Now, Christ makes himself the price of our redemption. In other words, he is our redemption money ; be buys us out from under the law, by paying himself as a ransom.   Christ hath redeemed us from the curse of the law, being made a curse for us ; and thus, also, redeems us from the power of sin.   But I must leave this train of thought, and return to a consideration of the plan of salvation.

Under this covenant of grace, our own works, or any thing that we do, or can do, as works of law, have no more to do with our salvation, than if we had never existed.   I wish your minds to separate entirely between salvation by works, and salvation by grace,   Our salvation by grace is founded on a reason entirely separate from and out of ourselves.   Before, it depended on ourselves.   Now we receive salvation, as a free gift, solely on account of Jesus Christ.   He is the sole author, ground, and reason of our salvation.   Whether we love God or do not love God so far as it is a ground of our salvation, is of no account.   The whole is entirely a matter of grace, through Jesus Christ. You will not understand me as saying that there is no necessity for love to God or good works.   I know that "without holiness no man shall see the Lord."   But the necessity of holiness is not at all on this ground.   Our own holiness does not enter at all into the ground or reason for our acceptance and salvation.   We are not going to be indebted to Christ for a while, until we are sanctified, and and all the rest of the time stand in our own righteousness. But however perfect and holy we may become, in this life, or to all eternity, Jesus Christ will for ever be the sole reason in the universe why we are not in hell.   Because, however holy we may become, it will be forever true that we have sinned, and in the eye of justice, nothing in us, short of our eternal damnation can satisfy the law.   But now, Jesus Christ has undertaken to help, and he for ever remains the sole ground of our salvation.

According to this plan, we have the benefit of his obedience to the law, just as if he had obeyed for us. Not that he did obey for us, in the distinction from himself, but we have the benefits of his obedience, by the gift of grace, the same as if he had done so.

I meant to dwell on the idea of Christ as our " Light," and our " Life," and our " Strength." But I perceive there is not time to-night. I wish to touch a little on this question, " How does faith put us in possession of Christ, in all these relations ? "

Faith in Christ puts us in possession of Christ, as the sum and substance of the blessings of the gospel. Christ was the very blessing promised in the Abrahamic covenant. And throughout the scriptures he is held forth as the sum and substance of all God's favors to man. He is " the Bread of Life," " the Water of Life," " our Strength," " our All," The gospel has taxed all the powers of language to describe the vast variety of his relations, and to show that faith is to put believers in possession of Jesus Christ, in all these relations.

The manner in which faith puts the mind in possession of all these blessings is this : It annihilates all those things that stand in the way of our intercourse with Christ. He says, " Behold, I stand at the door and knock, if any man hear my voice and open the door, I will come in to him, and will sup with him, and he with me." Here is a door, an obstacle to our intercourse with Christ, something that stands in the way. Take the particular of wisdom. Why do we not receive Christ as our wisdom ? Because we depend on our own wisdom, and think we have ourselves some available knowledge of the things of God, and as long as we depend on this we keep the door shut. That is the door. Now, let us just throw this all away, and give up all wisdom of our own, and see how infinitely empty we are of any available knowledge, as much so as a beast that perisheth, as to the way of salvation, until Christ shall teach us. Until we feel this, there is a door between us and Christ. We have something of our own, instead of coming and throwing ourselves perfectly into the hands of Christ, we just come to him to help out our own wisdom.

How does faith put us in possession of the righteousness of Christ? This is the way. Until our mind takes hold of the righteousness of Christ, we are alive to our own righteousness. We are naturally engaged in working out a righteousness of our own, and until we cease entirely from our own works, by absolutely throwing ourselves on Christ for righteousness, we do not come to Christ. Christ will not patch up our own righteousness, to make it answer the purpose. If we depend on our prayers, our tears, our charities, or anything we have done, or expect to do, he will not receive us. We must have none of this. But the moment an individual takes hold on Christ, he receives and appropriates all Christ's righteousness as his own ; as a perfect and unchangeable reason for his acceptance with God, by grace.

It is just so with regard to sanctification and redemption. I cannot dwell on them so particularly as I wished. Until an individual receives Christ, he does not cease from his own works. The moment he does that, by this very act he throws the entire responsibility upon Christ. The moment the mind does fairly yield itself up to Christ, the responsibility comes upon him, just as the person who undertakes to conduct a blind man is responsible for his safe conduct. The believer, by the act of faith, pledges Christ for his obedience and sanctification. By giving himself up to Christ, all the veracity of the Godhead is put at stake, that he shall be led right and made holy.

And with regard to redemption, as long as the sinner supposes that his own sufferings, his prayers, or tears, or mental agony, are of any avail, he will never receive Christ. But as soon as he receives Christ, he sinks down as lost and condemned—as in fact a dead person, unless redeemed by Christ.

CONCLUSION

I. There is no such thing as spiritual life in us, or anything acceptable to God, until we actually believe in Christ.

The very act of believing, receives Christ as just that influence which alone can wake up the mind to spiritual life.

II. We are nothing, as Christians, any farther than we believe in Christ.

III. Many seem to be waiting to do something first, before they receive Christ.

Some wait to become more dead to the world. Some to get a broken heart. Some to get their doubts cleared up before they come to Christ. *This is a grand mistake.* It is expecting to do that first, before faith, which is only the result of faith. Your heart will not be broken, your doubts will not be cleared up, you will never die to the world, until you believe. The moment you grasp the things of Christ, your mind will see, as in the light of eternity, the emptiness of the world, of reputation, riches, honor, and pleasure. To expect this first, preparatory to the exercise of faith, is beginning at the wrong end. It is seeking that as a preparation for faith, which is always the result of faith.

IV. Perfect faith will produce perfect love.

When the mind duly recognizes Christ, and receives him, in his various relations ; when the faith is unwavering and the views clear, there will be nothing left in the mind contrary to the law of God.

V. Abiding faith would produce abiding love.

Faith increasing, would produce increasing love. And here you ought to observe, that love may be perfect at all times, and yet be in different degrees at different times. An individual may love God perfectly and eternally, and yet his love may increase in vigor to all eternity, as I suppose it will. As the saints in glory see more and more of God's excellences, they will love him more and more, and yet will have perfect love all the time. That is, there will be nothing inconsistent with love in the mind, while the degrees of love will be different as their views of the character of God unfold. As God opens to their view the wonders of his glorious benevolence, they will have their souls thrilled with new love to God. In this life, the exercises of love vary greatly in degree. Sometimes God unfolds to his saints the wonders of his government, and gives them such views as well-nigh prostrate the body, and then love is greatly raised in degree. And yet the love may have been perfect before ; that is, the love of God was supreme and single, without any mixture of inconsistent affections. And it is not unreasonable to suppose, that it will be so to all eternity ; that occasions will occur in which the love of the saints will be brought into more lively exercise by new unfoldings of God's glory. As God develops to them wonder after wonder, their love will be increased indefinitely, and they will have continually enlarged accessions of its strength and fervor, to all eternity.

I designed to mention some things on the subject of instantaneous and progressive sanctification. But there is not time to-night, and they must be postponed.

VI. You see, beloved, from this subject, the way in which you can be made holy, and when you can be sanctified.

Whenever you come to Christ, and receive him for all that he is, and accept a whole salvation by grace, you will have all that Christ is to you, wisdom, and righteousness, and sanctification, and redemption. There is nothing but unbelief to hinder you from now enjoying it all. You need not wait for any preparation. There is no preparation that is of any avail. You must *receive* a whole salvation, as a *free gift*. When will you thus lay hold on Christ? When will you believe? Faith, true faith, always works by love, and purifies the heart, and overcomes the world. Whenever you find any difficulty in your way, you may know what is the matter. It is a want of faith. No matter what may befal you outwardly : if you find yourself thrown back in religion, or your mind thrown all into confusion, unbelief is the cause, and faith the remedy. If you lay hold on Christ, and keep hold, all the devils in hell can never drive you away from God, or put out your light. But if you let unbelief prevail, you may go on in this miserable, halting way, talking about sanctification, using words without knowledge, and dishonoring God, till you die.

5

LEGAL EXPERIENCE

The Seventh Chapter of the Epistle to the Romans

I HAVE more than once had occasion to refer to this chapter, and have read some portions of it and made remarks. But I have not been able to go into a consideration of it so fully as I wished, and therefore thought I would make it the subject of a separate lecture. In giving my views I shall pursue the following order :

I. Mention the different opinions that have prevailed in the church concerning this passage.

II. Show the importance of understanding this portion of scripture aright, or of knowing which of these prevailing opinions is the true one.

III. Lay down several facts and principles which have a bearing on the exposition of this passage.

IV. Refer to some rules of interpretation which ought always to be observed in interpreting either the Scriptures or any other writing or testimony.

V. Give my own views of the real meaning of the passage, with the reasons.

I shall confine myself chiefly to the latter part of the chapter, as that has been chiefly the subject of dispute. You see from the manner in which I have laid out my work, that I design to simplify the subject as much as possible, so as to bring it within the compass of a single lecture. Otherwise I might make a volume, so much having been written to show the meaning of this chapter.

I. I am to show what are the principal opinions that have prevailed concerning the application of this chapter.

1. One opinion that has extensively prevailed, and still prevails, is, that the latter part of the chapter is an epitome of Christian experience.

It has been supposed to describe the situation and exercises of a Christian, and designed to exhibit the christian warfare with indwelling sin. It is to be observed, howevei, that this is, comparatively, a modern opinion. No writer is known to have held this view of the chapter, for centuries after it was written. According to Professor Stuart, who has ·examined the subject more thoroughly than any other man in America, Augustine was the first writer that exhibited this interpretation, and he resorted to it in his controversy with Pelagius.

2. The only other interpretation given is that which prevailed in the first centuries, and which is still generally adopted on the continent of Europe, as well as by a con- siderable number of writers in England and in America, that this passage describes the experience of a sinner under conviction, who was acting under the motives of the law, and not yet brought to the experience of the gospel. In this country, the most prevalent opinion is, that the seventh chapter of Romans delineates the experience of a Christian.

II. I am to show the importance of a right understanding of this passage.

A right understanding of this passage must be funda- mental. If this passage in fact describes a sinner under conviction, or a purely legal experience, and if a person supposing that it is a Christian experience, finds his own experience to correspond with it, his mistake is a fatal one. It must be a fatal error, to rest in his experience as that of a real Christian, because it corresponds with the seventh of Romans, if Paul in fact is giving only the experience of a sinner under legal motives and considerations.

III. I will lay down some principles and facts that have a bearing on the elucidation of this subject.

1. It is true that mankind act, in all cases, and from the nature of mind, must always act, as on the whole they feel to be preferable.

Or, in other words, the will governs the conduct. Men never act against their will. The will governs the motion of the limbs. Voluntary beings cannot act contrary to their will.

2. Men often desire what, on the whole they do not choose.

The desires and the will are often opposed to each other. The conduct is governed by the choice, not by the desires. The desires may be inconsistent with the choice. You may desire to go to some other place to-night, and yet on the whole choose to remain here. Perhaps you desire very strongly to be somewhere else, and yet choose to remain in meeting. A man wishes to go a journey to some place. Perhaps he desires it strongly. It may be very important to his business or his ambition. But his family are sick, or some other object requires him to be at home, and on the whole he chooses to remain. In all cases, the conduct follows the actual choice.

3. Regeneration, or conversion, is a change in the choice.

It is a change in the supreme controlling choice of the mind. The regenerated or converted person prefers God's glory to everything else. He chooses it as the supreme object of affection. This is a change of heart. Before, he chose his own interest or happiness, as his supreme end. Now, he chooses God's service in preference to his own interest. When a person is truly born again, his choice is habitually right, and of course his conduct is in the main right.

The force of temptation may produce an occasional wrong choice, or even a succession of wrong choices, but his habitual course of action is right. The will, or choice, of a converted person is habitually right, and of course his conduct is so. If this is not true, I ask, in what does the converted differ from the unconverted person? If it is not the character of the converted person, that he habitually does the commandments of God, what is his character? But I presume this position will not be disputed by any one who believes in the doctrine of regeneration.

4. Moral agents are so constituted, that they naturally and necessarily approve of what is right.

A moral agent is one who possesses understanding, will, and conscience. Conscience is the power of discerning the difference of moral objects. It will not be disputed that a moral agent can be led to see the difference between right and wrong, so that his moral nature shall approve of what is right. Otherwise, a sinner never can be brought under conviction. If he has not a moral nature, that can see and highly approve the law of God, and justify the penalty, he cannot be convicted. For this is conviction, to see the goodness of the law that he has broken and the justice of the penalty he has incurred. But in fact, there is not a moral agent, in heaven, earth, or hell, that cannot be made to see that the law of God is right, and whose conscience does not approve the law.

5. Men may not only approve the law, as right, but they may often, when it is viewed abstractly and without reference to its bearing on themselves, take real pleasure in contemplating it.

This is one great source of self-deception. Men view the law of God in the abstract, and love it. When no selfish reason is present for opposing it, they take pleasure in viewing it. They approve of what is right, and condemn wickedness, in the abstract. All men do this, when no selfish reason is pressing on them. Who ever found a man so wicked, that he approved of evil in the abstract? Where was a moral being ever found that approved the character of the devil, or that approved of other wicked men, unconnected with himself ?   How often do you hear wicked men express the greatest abhorrence and detestation of enormous wickedness in others.   If their passions are in no way enlisted in favor of error or of wrong, men always stand up for what is right.   And this merely constitutional approbation of what is right, may amount even to delight, when they do not see the relations of right interfering in any manner with their own selfishness.

6. In this constitutional approbation of truth and the law of God, and the delight which naturally arises from it, there is no virtue.

It is only what belongs to man's moral nature.   It arises naturally from the constitution of the mind.   Mind is constitutionally capable of seeing the beauty of virtue. And so far from there being any virtue in it, it is in fact only a clearer proof of the strength of their depravity, that when they know the right, and see its excellence, they do not obey it.   It is not then that impenitent sinners have in them something that is holy.   But their wickedness is herein seen to be so much the greater.   For the wickedness of sin is in proportion to the light that is enjoyed. And when we find that men may not only see the excellence of the law of God, but even strongly approve of it and take delight in it, and yet not obey it, it shows how desperately wicked they are, and makes sin appear exceeding sinful.

7. It is a common use of language for persons to say, "I would do so and so, but cannot," when they only mean to be understood as desiring it, but not as actually choosing to do it.   And so to say, "I could not do so," when they only mean that they would not do it, and, they could if they would.

Not long since, I asked a minister to preach for me next Sabbath.   He answered, "I can't."   I found out afterwards that he could if he would. I asked a merchant to take a certain price for a piece of goods. He said, " I can't do it." What did he mean ? That he had not power to accept of such a price ? Not at all. He could if he would, but he did not choose to do it. You will see the bearing of these remarks, when I come to read the chapter. I proceed now.

IV. To give several rules of interpretation, that are aplicable to the interpretation not only of the Bible, but of all written instruments, and to all evidence whatever.

There are certain rules of evidence which all men are bound to apply, in ascertaining the meaning of instruments and the testimony of witnesses, and of all writings.

1. We are always to put that construction on language which is required by the nature of the subject.

We are bound always to understand a person's language as it is applicable to the subject of discourse. Much of the language of common life may be tortured into any thing, if you lose sight of the subject, and take the liberty to interpret it without reference to what they are speaking of. How much injury has been done, by interpreting separate passages and single expressions in the scriptures, in violation of this principle. It is chiefly by overlooking this simple rule, that the scriptures have been tortured into the support of errors and contradictions innumerable and absurd beyond all calculation. This rule is applicable to all statements. Courts of justice never would allow such perversions as have been committed upon the Bible.

2. If a person's language will admit, we are bound always to construe it so as to make him consistent with himself.

Unless you observe this rule, you can scarcely converse five minutes with any individual on any subject and not make him contradict himself. If you do not hold to this rule, how can one man ever communicate his ideas so that another man will understand them ? How can a witness ever make known the facts to the jury, if his language is to be tortured at pleasure, without the restraints of this rule ?

3. In interpreting a person's language, we are always to keep in view the point to which he is speaking.

We are to understand the scope of his argument, the object he has in view, and the point to which he is speaking. Otherwise we shall of course not understand his language. Suppose I were to take up a book, any book, and not keep my eye on the object the writer had in view in making it, and the point at which he is aiming, I never can understand that book. It is easy to see how endless errors have grown out of a practice of interpreting the Scriptures in disregard of the first principles of interpretation.

4. When you understand the point to which a person is speaking, you are to understand him as speaking to that point ; and not put a construction on his language unconnected with his object, or inconsistent with it.

By losing sight of this rule, you may make nonsense of every thing. You are bound always to interpret language in the light of the subject to which it is applied, or about which it is spoken.

V. Having laid down these rules and principles, I proceed, in the light of them, to give my own view of the meaning of the passage, with the reasons for it. But first I will make a remark or two.

1st. Remark. Whether the apostle was speaking of himself in this passage, or whether he is supposing a case, is not material to the right interpretation of the language.

It is supposed by many, that because he speaks in the first person, he is to be understood as referring to himself. But it is a common practice, when we are discussing general principles, or arguing a point, to suppose a case by way of illustration, or to establish a point. And it is very natural to state it in the first person, without at all intending to be understood, and in fact without ever being understood, as declaring an actual occurrence, or an experience of our own. The apostle Paul was here pursuing a close train of argument, and he introduces this simply by way of illustration. And it is no way material whether it is his own actual experience, or a case supposed.

If he is speaking of himself, or if he is speaking of another person, or if he is supposing a case, he does it with a design to show a general principle of conduct, and that all persons under like circumstances would do the same. Whether he is speaking of a Christian, or of an impenitent sinner, he lays down a general principle.

The apostle James, in the 3d chapter, speaks in the first person ; even in administering reproof. " My brethren, be not many masters, knowing that we shall receive the greater condemnation. For in many things we offend all."

" Therewith bless we God, even the Father ; and therewith curse we men, which are made after the similitude of God."

The apostle Paul often says, " I," and uses the first person, when discussing and illustrating general principles : " All things are lawful unto me, but all things are not expedient : all things are lawful for me, but I will not be brought under the power of any." And again, " Conscience, I say, not thine own, but of the other : for why is my liberty judged of another man's conscience ? For if I by grace be a partaker, why am I evil spoken of for that for which I give thanks ? For now we see through a glass, darkly ; but then face to face : now I know in part ; but then shall I know even as also I am known. And now abideth faith, hope, charity, these three ; but the greatest of these is charity." So also, " For if I build again the things which I destroyed, I make myself a transgressor." In 1st Cor. iv. 6. he explains exactly how he uses illustrations, "And these things, brethren, I have in a figure transferred to myself, and to Apollos, for your sakes : that ye might learn in us not to think of men above that which is written, that no one of you be puffed up for one against another."

2d Remark. Much of the language which the apostle uses here, is applicable to the case of a backslider, who has lost all but the form of religion. He has left his first love, and has in fact fallen under the influence of legal motives, of hope and fear, just like an impenitent sinner. If there be such a character as a real backslider, who has been a real convert, he is then actuated by the same motives as the sinner, and the same language may be equally applicable to both. And therefore the fact that some of the language before us is applicable to a Christian who has become a backslider, does not prove at all that the experience here described is Christian experience, but only that a backslider and a sinner are in many respects alike. I do not hesitate to say this much, at least : that no one, who was conscious that he was actuated by love to God could ever have thought of applying this chapter to himself. If any one is not in the exercise of love to God, this describes his character ; and whether he is blackslider or sinner, it is all the same thing.

3d Remark. Some of the expressions here used by the apostle are supposed to describe the case of a believer who is not an habitual backslider, but who is overcome by temptation and passion for a time, and speaks of himself as if he were all wrong. A man is tempted, we are told, when he is drawn away by his own lusts, and enticed. And in that state, no doubt, he might find expressions here that would describe his own experience, while under such influence. But that proves nothing in regard to the de-

sign of the passage, for while he is in this state, he is so
far under a certain influence, and the impenitent sinner is
all the time under just such influence. The same language, therefore, may be applicable to both, without in-
consistency.

But although some expressions may bear this plausible
construction, yet a view of the whole passage makes it
evident that it cannot be a delineation of Christian experience. My own opinion therefore is, that the apostle designed here to represent the experience of a sinner, not
careless, but strongly convicted, and yet not converted.
The reasons are these :

1. Because the apostle is here manifestly describing the
habitual character of some one ; and this one is wholly
under the dominion of the flesh. It is not as a whole a
description of one who, under the power of present temptation, is acting inconsistently with his general character,
but his general character is so. It is one who uniformly
falls into sin, notwithstanding his approval of the law.

2. It would have been entirely irrelevant to his purpose, to state the experience of a Christian as an illustration of his argument. That was not what was needed.
He was laboring to vindicate the law of God, in its influence on a carnal mind. In a previous chapter he had
stated the fact, that justification was only by faith, and not
by works of law. In this seventh chapter, he maintains not
only that *justification* is by faith, but also that *sanctification* is only by faith. " Know ye not brethren, (for I speak
to them that know the law) how that the law hath dominion over a man as long as he liveth ? So then, if
while her husband liveth, she be married to another man,
she shall be called an adulteress ; but if her husband be
dead, she is free from that law ; so that she is no adulteress,
though she be married to another man." What is the use
of all this ? Why, this, " Wherefore, my brethren, ye also

are become dead to the law by the body of Christ ; that ye should be married to another, even to him who is raised from the dead, that we should bring forth fruit unto God." While you were under the law you were bound to obey the law, and hold to the terms of the law for justification. But now being made free from the law, as a rule of judgment, you are no longer influenced by legal considerations, of hope and fear, for Christ to whom you are married, has set aside the penalty, that by faith ye might be justified before God.

" For when we were in the flesh," that is, in an unconverted state, " the motions of sins, which were by the law, did work in our members to bring forth fruit unto death . But now we are delivered from the law, that being dead wherein we were held ; that we should serve in newness of spirit, and not in the oldness of the letter." Here he is stating the real condition of a Christian, that he serves in newness of spirit and not in the oldness of the letter.   He had found that the fruit of the law was only death and by the gospel he had been brought into true subjection to Christ.   What is the objection to this ?   " What shall we say then ?   Is the law sin ?   God forbid.   Nay, I had not known sin, but by the law : for I had not known lust, except the law had said, Thou shalt not covet.   And the commandment which was ordained to life, I found to be unto death."   The law was enacted that people might live by it, if they would perfectly obey it ; but when we were in the flesh, we found it unto death.   " For sin, taking occasion by the commandment, deceived me, and by it slew me.   Wherefore the law is holy, and the commandment holy, and just, and good."   Now he brings up the objection again.   How can anything that is good be made death unto you ?   " Was, then, that which is good made death unto me ?   God forbid.   But sin, that it might appear sin, working death in me by that which is good ; that sin by the commandment might be exceeding sinful." And he vindicates the law, by showing that it is not the fault of the law, but the fault of sin, and that this very result shows at once the excellence of the law and the exceeding sinfulness of sin. Sin must be a horrible thing, if it can work such a perversion, as to take the good law of God and make it the means of death.

" For we know that the law is spiritual ; but I am carnal, sold under sin." Here is the hinge, on which the whole questions turns. Now mark ; the apostle is here vindicating the law against the objection, that if the law is means of death to sinners it cannot be good. Against this objection, he goes to show, that all its action on the mind of the sinner proves it to be good. Keeping his eye on this point, he argues, that the law is good, and that the evil comes from the motions of sin in our members. Now he comes to that part which is supposed to delineate a Christian experience, and which is the subject of controversy. He begins by saying "the law is spiritual but I am carnal." This word "carnal" he uses once, and only once, in reference to Christians, and then it was in reference to persons who were in a low state in religion. "For ye are yet carnal ; for whereas there is among you envying, and strife, and divisions, are ye not carnal, and walk as men." These Christians had backslidden, and acted as if they were not converted persons, but were carnal. The term itself is generally used to signify the worst of sinners. Paul here defines it so ; " carnal, sold under sin." Could that be said of Paul himself, at the time he wrote this epistle ? Was that his own experience ? Was he sold under sin ? Was that true of the great apostle ? No, but he was vindicating the law, and he uses an illustration, by supposing a case. He goes on, " For that which I do, I allow not ; for what I would, that I do not ; but what I hate, that do I."

Here you see the application of the principles I have laid down. In the interpretation of this word "would," we are not to understand it of the choice or will, but only a desire. Otherwise the apostle contradicts a plain matter of fact, which every body knows to be true, that the will governs the conduct. Professor Stuart has very properly rendered the word desire ; what I desire, I do not, but what I disapprove, that I do. Then comes the conclusion, "If, then, I do that which I would not, I consent unto the law, that it is good. "If I do that which I disapprove, if I disapprove of my own conduct, if I condemn myself, I thereby bear testimony that the law is good. Now, keep your eye on the object the apostle has in view and read the next verse, "Now then it is no more I that do it, but sin that dwelleth in me." Here he, as it were, divides himself against himself, or speaks of himself as possessing two natures, or, as some of the heathen philosophers taught, as having two souls, one which approves the good and another which loves and chooses evil. "For I know that in me (that is, in my flesh) dwelleth no good thing : for to will is present with me ; but how to perform that which is good I find not." Here "to will" means to approve, for if men really *will* to do a thing, they do it. This everybody knows. Where the language will admit, we are bound to interpret it so as to make it consistent with known facts. If you understand "to will" literally, you involve the apostle in the absurdity of saying that he willed what he did not do, and so acted contrary to his own will, which contradicts a notorious fact. The meaning must be desire. Then it coincides with the experience of every convicted sinner. He knows what he ought to do, and he strongly approves it, but he is not ready to do it. Suppose I were to call on you to do some act. Suppose, for instance, I were to call on those of you who are impenitent, to come forward and take that seat, that we might see who you are, and pray for you, and should show you your sins and that it is your duty to submit to God, some of you would exclaim, "I know it is my duty, and I greatly desire to do it, but I cannot." What do you mean by it? Why, simply, that on the whole, the balance of your will is on the other side.

In the 20th verse he repeats what he had said before, "Now if I do that I would not, it is no more I that do it, but sin that dwelleth in me." Is that the habitual character and experience of a Christian? I admit that a Christian may fall so low that this language may apply to him; but if this is his general character, how does it differ from that of an impenitent sinner? If this is the habitual character of a Christian, there is not a word of truth in the scripture representations, that the saints are those who really obey God; for here is one called a Christian, of whom it is said expressly that he never does obey.

"I find then a law, that when I would do good, evil is present with me." Here he speaks of the action of the carnal propensities, as being so constant and so prevalent that he calls it a "law." "For I delight in the law of God after the inward man." Here is the great stumbling-block. Can it be said of an impenitent sinner that he "delights" in the law of God? I answer, Yes. I know the expression is strong, but the apostle was using strong language all along, on both sides. It is no stronger language than the prophet Isaiah uses in chapter lviii. He was describing as wicked and rebellious a generation as ever lived. He says, "Cry aloud, spare not; lift up thy voice like a trumpet, and show my people their transgression, and the house of Jacob their sins." Yet he goes on to say of this very people, "Yet they seek me daily, and delight to know my ways, as a nation that did righteousness, and forsook not the ordinance of their God; they ask of me the ordinances of justice; they *take delight* in approaching to God." Here is one instance of impenitent sinners manifestly delighting in approaching to God. So in Ezekiel xxxiii. 32. "And lo thou art unto them as a very lovely song of one that hath a pleasant voice, and can play well on an instrument : for they hear thy words, but do them not." The prophet had been telling how wicked they were. "And they come unto thee as the people cometh, and they sit before thee as my people, and they hear thy words, but they will not do them: for with their mouth they show much love, but their heart goeth after their covetousness." Here were impenitent sinners, plainly enough, yet they love to hear the eloquent prophet. How often do ungodly sinners delight in eloquent preaching or powerful reasoning, by some able minister ! It is to them an intellectual feast. And sometimes they are so pleased with it, as really to think they love the word of God. This is consistent with entire depravity of heart, and enmity against the true character of God. Nay, it sets their depravity in a stronger light, because they know and approve the right, and yet do the wrong.

So, notwithstanding this delight in the law, he says, "But I see another law in my members, warring against the law of my mind, and bringing me into captivity to the law of sin which is in my members. O wretched man that I am ! who shall deliver me from the body of this death ?" Here the words, "I thank God, through Jesus Christ our Lord," are plainly a parenthesis, and a break in upon the train of thought, Then he sums up the whole matter, "So then, with the mind I myself serve the law of God, but with the flesh the law of sin."

It is as if he had said, My better self, my unbiased judgment, my conscience, approves the law of God ; but the law in my members, my passions, have such a control over me, that I still disobey. Remember, the apostle was describing the habitual character of one who was wholly under the dominion of sin. It was irrelevant to his purpose to adduce the experience of a Christian. He was vindicating the law, and therefore it was necessary for him to take the case of one who was under the law. If it is Christian experience, he was reasoning against himself; for if it is Christian experience, this would prove, not only that the law is inefficacious for the subduing of passion and the sanctification of men, but that the gospel also is inefficacious. Christians are under grace, and it is irrelevant, in vindicating the law, to adduce the experience of those who are not under the law, but under grace.

Another conclusive reason is, that he here actually states the case of a believer as entirely different. In verses four and six, he speaks of those who are not under law and not in the flesh; that is, not carnal, but delivered from the law, and actually serving, or obeying God, in spirit.

Then, in the beginning of the eighth chapter, he goes on to say, "There is therefore now no condemnation to them which are in Christ Jesus, who walk not after the flesh, but after the spirit. For the law of the Spirit of life in Christ Jesus, hath made me free from the law of sin and death." He had alluded to this in the parenthesis above, "I thank God," etc. "For what the law could not do, in that it was weak through the flesh, God sending his own Son in the flesh, and for sin, condemned sin in the flesh : that the righteousness of the law might be fulfilled in us who walk not after the flesh but after the Spirit." Who is this of whom he is now speaking? If the person in the last chapter was one who had a Christian experience—whose experience is this? Here is something entirely different. The other was wholly under the power of sin, and under the law, and while he knew his duty, never did it. Here we find one for whom what the law could not do, through the power of passion, the gospel has done, so that the righteousness of the law is fulfilled, or what the law requires is obeyed. "For they that are after the flesh, do mind the things of the flesh ; but they that are after the Spirit, the things of the Spirit. For to be carnally minded is death ; but to be spiritually-minded is life and peace : because the carnal mind is enmity to God : for it is not subject to the law of God, neither indeed can be. So then they that are in the flesh cannot please God." There it is. Those whom he had described in the seventh chapter, as being carnal, cannot please God. '· But ye are not in the flesh, but in the Spirit, if so be that the Spirit of God dwell in you. Now, if any man have not the Spirit of Christ, he is none of his. And if Christ be in you, the body is dead because of sin ; but the Spirit is life because of righteousness." But here is an individual whose body is dead. Before the body had the control, and dragged him away from duty and from salvation ; but now the power of passion is subdued.

Now I will give you the sum of the whole matter :

(1.) The strength of the apostle's language cannot decide this question, for he uses strong language on both sides. If it be objected that the individual he is descriving is said to "delight in the law, " he is also said to be "carnal, sold under sin." When a writer uses strong language, it must be so understood as not to make it irrelevant or inconsistent.

(2.) Whether he spoke of himself, or of some other person, or merely supposed a case by way of illustration, is wholly immaterial to the question.

(3.) It is plain that the point he wished to illustrate was the vindication of the law of God, as to its influence on a carnal mind.

(4.) The point required by way of illustration, the case of a convicted sinner, who saw the excellence of the law, but in whom the passions had the ascendancy.

(5.) If this is spoken of Christian experience, it is not

only irrelevant, but proves the reverse of what he intended. He intended to show that the law though good, could not break the power of passion. But if this is Christian experience, then it proves that the gospel, instead of the law cannot subdue passion and sanctify men.

(6.) The contrast between the state described in the seventh chapter, and that described in the eighth chapter, proves that the experience of the former was not that of a Christian.

CONCLUSION

I. Those who find their own experience written in the seventh chapter of Romans, are not converted persons. If that is their habitual character, they are not regenerated ; they are under conviction, but not Christians.

II. You see the great importance of using the law in dealing with sinners, to make them prize the gospel, to lead them to justify God and condemn themselves. Sinners are never made truly to repent but as they are convicted by the law.

III. At the same time, you see the entire insufficiency of the law to convert men. The case of the devil illustrates the highest efficacy of the law, in this respect.

IV. You see the danger of mistaking mere desires for piety. Desire, that does not result in right choice, has nothing good in it. The devil may have such desires. The wickedest men on earth may desire religion, and no doubt often do desire it, when they see that it is necessary to their salvation, or to control their passions.

V. Christ and the gospel present the only motives that can sanctify the mind. The law only convicts and condemns.

VI. Those who are truly converted and brought into the liberty of the gospel, do find deliverance from the bondage of their own corruptions.

They do find the power of the body over the mind broken. They may have conflicts and trials, many and severe ; but as an habitual thing, they are delivered from the thraldom of passion, and get the victory over sin, and find it easy to serve God. His commandments are not grievous to them. His yoke is easy, and his burden light.

VII. The true convert finds peace with God. He feels that he has it. He enjoys it. He has a sense of pardoned sin, and of victory over corruption.

VIII. You see, from this subject, the true position of a vast many church members. They are all the while struggling under the law. They approve of the law, both in its precept and its penalty, they feel condemned, and desire relief. But still they are unhappy. They have no spirit of prayer, no communion with God, no evidence of adoption. They only refer to the 7th of Romans as their evidence. Such a one will say, "There is my experience exactly." Let me tell you, that if this is your experience, you are yet in the gall of bitterness and the bonds of iniquity. You feel that you are in the bonds of guilt, and you are overcome by iniquity, and surely you know that it is bitter as gall. Now, don't cheat your soul by supposing that with such an experience as this, you can go and sit down by the side of the apostle Paul. You are yet carnal, sold under sin, and unless you embrace the gospel, you will be damned.

6

CHRIST OUR ADVOCATE

"And if any man sin we have an Advocate with the Father, Jesus Christ, the righteous. And he is the propitiation for our sins: and not for ours only, but also for the sins of the whole world."—1 *John* ii. 1, 2

THE Bible abounds with governmental analogies. These are designed for our instruction; but if we receive instruction from them, it is because there is a real analogy in many points between the government of God and human governments.

I propose to inquire,—

I. What is the *idea* of an advocate when the term is used to express a governmental office or relation?

An advocate is one who pleads the cause of another; who represents another, and acts in his name; one who uses his influence in behalf of another by his request.

II. *Purposes for which an advocate may be employed.*

1. To secure justice, in case any question involving justice is to be tried.

2. To defend the accused. If one has been accused of committing a crime, an advocate may be employed to conduct his trial on his behalf; to defend him against the charge, and prevent his conviction if possible.

3. An advocate may be employed to secure a pardon, when a criminal has been justly condemned, and is under sentence. That is, an advocate may be employed either to secure *justice* for his client, or to obtain *mercy* for him, in case he is con-

demned; may be employed either to prevent his conviction,
or when convicted, may be employed in setting aside the
execution of the law upon the criminal.

III. *The sense in which Christ is the advocate of sinners.*

He is employed to plead the cause of sinners, not at the
bar of justice; not to defend them against the charge of sin,
because the question of their guilt is already settled. The
Bible represents them as condemned *already ;* and such is
the fact, as every sinner knows. Every sinner in the world
knows that he has sinned, and that consequently he must be
condemned by the law of God. This office, then, is exercised
by Christ in respect to sinners ; not at the bar of justice, but
at the throne of grace, at the footstool of sovereign mercy.
He is employed, not to prevent the *conviction* of the sinner,
but to prevent his *execution ;* not to prevent his being condemned, but being already condemned, to prevent his being
damned.

IV. What is implied in His being the *Advocate* of sinners.

1. His being employed at a throne of grace and not at the
bar of justice, to plead for *sinners*, as such, and not for those
who are merely charged with sin, but the charge not established. This implies that the guilt of the sinner is already
ascertained, the verdict of guilty given, the sentence of the
law pronounced, and that the sinner awaits his execution.

2. His being appointed by God as the Advoca e of sinners implies a merciful disposition in God. If God had not
been mercifully disposed towards sinners, no Advocate had
been appointed, no question of forgiveness had been
raised.

3. It implies also that the exercise of mercy on certain
conditions is *possible.* Not only is God mercifully disposed,
but to *manifest* this disposition in the actual pardon of sin is
possible. Had not this been the case, no Advocate had been
appointed.

4. It implies that there is hope, then, for the condemned.

Sinners are prisoners; but in this world they are not yet prisoners of despair, but are prisoners of hope.

5. It implies that there is a governmental necessity for the interposition of an advocate; that the sinner's relations are such, and his character such, that he can not be admitted to plead his own cause in his own name. He is condemned, he is no longer on trial. In this respect he is under sentence for a capital crime; consequently he is an outlaw, and the government can not recognize him as being capable of performing any legal act. His relations to the government forbid that in his own name, or in his own person, he should appear before God. So far as his own personal influence with the government is concerned, he is as a dead man—he is *civilly* dead. Therefore, he must appear by his next friend, or by his advocate, if he is heard at all. He may not appear in his own name and in his own person, but must appear by an advocate who is acceptable to the government.

V. I next call attention to the *essential qualifications* of an advocate under such circumstances.

1. He must be the uncompromising friend of the government. Observe, he appears to pray for mercy to be extended to the guilty party whom he represents. Of course he must not himself be the enemy of the government of whom he asks so great a favor; but he should be known to be the devoted friend of the government whose mercy he prays may be extended to the guilty.

2. He must be the uncompromising friend of the dishonored law. The sinner has greatly dishonored, and by his conduct denounced, both the law and the Law-giver. By his uniform disobedience the sinner has proclaimed, in the most emphatic manner, that the law is not worthy of obedience, and that the Law-giver is a tyrant. Now the Advocate must be a *friend* to this law; he must not sell himself to the dishonor of the law nor consent to its dishonor. He must

not *reflect* upon the law; for in this case he places the Law-giver in a position in which, if he should set aside the penalty and exercise mercy, he would consent to the dishonor of the law, and by a public act himself condemn the law. The Advocate seeks to dispense with the execution of the law; but he must not offer, as a reason, that the law is unreasonable and unjust. For in this case he renders it impossible for the Law-giver to set aside the execution without consenting to the assertion that the law is not good. In that case the Law-giver would condemn himself instead of the sinner. It is plain, then, that he must be the uncompromising friend of the law, or he can never secure the exercise of mercy without involving the Law-giver himself in the crime of dishonoring the law.

3. The Advocate must be *righteous ;* that is, he must be clear of any complicity in the crime of the sinner. He must have no fellowship with his crime; there must be no *charge* or *suspicion* of guilt resting upon the Advocate. Unless he himself be clear of the crime of which the criminal is accused, he is not the proper person to represent him before a throne of mercy.

4. He must be the *compassionate friend* of the sinner—not of his *sins*, but of the sinner himself. This distinction is very plain. Every one knows that a parent can be greatly opposed to the wickedness of his children, while he has great compassion for their person. He is not a true friend to the sinner who really sympathizes with his sins. I have several times heard sinners render as an excuse for not being Christians, that their friends were opposed to it. They have a great many dear friends who are opposed to their becoming Christians and obeying God. They desire them to live on in their sins. They do not want them to change and become holy, but desire them to remain in their worldly-mindedness and sinfulness. I tell such persons that those are their friends in the same sense that the devil is their friend.

And would they call the devil their good friend, their kind friend, because he sympathizes with their sins, and wishes them not to become Christians? Would you call a man your friend, who wished you to commit murder, or robbery, to tell a lie, or commit any crime? Suppose he should come and appeal to you, and because you are his friend should desire you to commit some great crime, would you regard that man as your friend?

No! No man is a true friend of a sinner, unless he is desirous that he should abandon his sins. If any person would have you continue in your sins, he is the adversary of your soul. Instead of being in any proper sense your friend, he is playing the devil's part to ruin you.

Now *observe :* Christ is the compassionate friend of sinners, a friend in the best and truest sense. He does not sympathize with your sins, but His heart is set upon saving you from your sins. I said He must be the *compassionate* friend of sinners; and His compassion must be stronger than death, or He will never meet the necessities of the case.

5. Another qualification must be, that He is able sufficiently to honor the law, which sinners by their transgression have dishonored. He seeks to avoid the execution of the dishonored law of God. The law having been dishonored by sin in the highest degree, must either be honored by its execution on the criminal, or the Law-giver must in some other way bear testimony in favor of the law, before He can justly dispense with the execution of its penalty. The law is not to be repealed ; the law must not be dishonored. It is the law of God's nature, the unalterable law of His government, the eternal law of heaven, the law for the government of moral agents in all worlds, and in all time, and to all eternity. Sinners have borne their most emphatic testimony against it, by pouring contempt upon it in utterly refusing to obey it. Now sin must not be treated lightly this law must be honored.

God might pour a flash of glory over it by executing its
penalty upon the whole race that have despised it. This
would be the solemn testimony of God to sustain its authority and vindicate its claims. If our Advocate appears before
God to ask for the remission of sin, that the penalty of this
law may be set aside and not executed, the question immediately arises, But how shall the *dishonor* of this law be
avoided? What shall compensate for the reckless and blas-
phemous contempt with which this law has been treated?
How shall sin be forgiven without apparently making light
of it?

It is plain that sin has placed the whole question in such a
light that God's testimony must in some way be borne in a
most emphatic manner against sin, and to sustain the authority of this dishonored law.

It behooves the Advocate of sinners to provide Himself
with a plea that shall meet this difficulty. He must meet
this necessity, if He would secure the setting aside of the
penalty. He must be able to provide an adequate substitute
for its execution. He must be able to do that which will as
effectually bear testimony in favor of the law and against sin
as the execution of the law upon the criminal would do. In
other words, He must be able to meet the demands of public justice.

6. He must be willing to *volunteer* a *gratuitous* service.
He can not be called upon in *justice* to *volunteer* a service,
or suffer for the sake of sinners. He may volunteer His
service and it may be accepted; but if He does volunteer
His service, He must be able and willing to endure whatever
pain or sacrifice is necessary to meet the case.

If the law must be honored by obedience; if, " without
the shedding of blood, there can be no remission;" if an
emphatic governmental testimony must be borne against sin,
and in honor of the law; if He must become the representative of sinners, offering Himself before the whole universe as

a propitiation for sin, He must be willing to meet the case and make the sacrifice.

7. He must have a good plea. In other words, when He appears before the mercy-seat, He must be able to present such considerations as shall really meet the necessities of the case, and render it safe, proper, honorable, glorious in God to forgive.

VI. I now come to inquire *what His plea in behalf of sinners is.* It should be remembered that the appeal is not to *justice.* Since the fall of man, God has plainly *suspended* the execution of strict justice upon our race. To us, as a matter of fact, He has set upon a throne of mercy. Mercy, and not justice, has been the rule of His administration, since men were involved in sin.

This is simple fact. Men do sin, and they are not cut off immediately and sent to hell. The execution of justice is suspended; and God is represented as seated upon a throne of grace, or upon a mercy-seat. It is here at a mercy-seat that Christ executes the office of Advocate for sinners.

2. Christ's plea for sinners can not be that they are not guilty. They are guilty, and condemned. No question can be raised as it respects their guilt and their ill-desert; such questions are settled. It has often appeared strange to me that men overlook the fact that they are condemned already, and that no question respecting their guilt or desert of punishment can ever be raised.

3. Christ as our Advocate can not, and need not, plead a *justification.* A plea of justification admits the *fact* charged; but asserts that under the circumstances the accused had a right to do as he did. This plea Christ can never make. This is entirely out of place, the case having been already tried, and sentence passed.

4. He may not plead what will *reflect*, in any wise, upon the law. He can not plead that the law was too strict in its precept, or too severe in its penalty; for in that case he would

not really plead for mercy, but for justice. He would plead in that case that no injustice might be done the criminal. For if he intimates that the law is not just, then the sinner does not deserve the punishment; hence it would be unjust to punish him, and his plea would amount to this, that the sinner be not punished, because he does not deserve it. But if this plea should be allowed to prevail, it would be a public acknowledgment on the part of God that His law was unjust. But this may never be.

5. He may not plead anything that shall reflect upon the *administration of the Law-giver*. Should he plead that men had been hardly treated by the Law-giver, either in their creation, or by His providential arrangements, or by suffering them to be so tempted—or if, in any wise, he brings forward a plea that reflects upon the Law-giver, in creation, or in the administration of His government, the Law-giver can not listen to his plea, and forgive the sinner, without condemning Himself. In that case, instead of insisting that the sinner should repent, virtually the Law-giver would be called upon *Himself* to repent.

6. He may not plead any *excuse whatever* for the sinner in mitigation of his guilt, or in extenuation of his conduct. For if he does, and the Law-giver should forgive in answer to such a plea, He would confess that He had been wrong, and that the sinner did not deserve the sentence that had been pronounced against him.

He must not plead that the sinner does not deserve the damnation of hell; for, should he urge this plea, it would virtually accuse the justice of God, and would be equivalent to begging that the sinner might not be sent unjustly to hell. This would not be a proper plea for mercy, but rather an issue with justice. It would be asking that the sinner might not be sent to hell, not because of the mercy of God, but because the justice of God forbids it. This will never be.

7. He can not plead as our Advocate that He has paid our

debt, in such a sense that He can demand our discharge on the ground of justice. He has not paid our debt in such a sense that we do not still owe it. He has not atoned for our sins in such a sense that we might not still be justly punished for them. Indeed, such a thing is impossible and absurd. One being can not suffer for another in such a sense as to remove the guilt of that other. He may suffer for another's guilt in such a sense that it will be safe to forgive the sinner, for whom the suffering has been endured; but the suffering of the substitute can never, in the least degree, diminish the intrinsic guilt of the criminal. Our Advocate may urge that He has borne such suffering for us to honor the law that we had dishonored, that now it is safe to extend mercy to us; but He never can demand our discharge on the ground that we do not *deserve* to be punished. The fact of our intrinsic guilt remains, and must forever remain; and our forgiveness is just as much an act of sovereign mercy, as if Christ had never died for us.

8. But Christ may plead His sin-offering to sanction the law, as fulfilling a condition, upon which we may be forgiven.

This offering is not to be regarded as the *ground* upon which justice demands our forgiveness. The appeal of our Advocate is not to this offering as payment in such a sense that now in justice He can *demand* that we shall be set free. No. As I said before, it is simply the fulfilling of a condition, upon which it is safe for the mercy of God to arrest and set aside the execution of the law, in the case of the penitent sinner.

Some theologians appear to me to have been unable to see this distinction. They insist upon it that the atonement of Christ is the *ground* of our forgiveness. They seem to assume that He *literally* bore the penalty for us in such a sense that Christ now no longer appeals to *mercy*, but demands *justice* for us. To be consistent they must maintain that Christ does not plead at a mercy-seat for us, but having paid our debt, appears before a throne of justice, and *demands* our discharge.

I cannot accept this view. I insist that His offering could not touch the question of our intrinsic desert of damnation. His appeal is to the infinite mercy of God, to His loving disposition to pardon; and He points to His atonement, not as demanding our release, but as fulfilling a condition upon which our release is honorable to God. His obedience to the law and the shedding of His blood He may plead as a substitute for the execution of the law upon us—in short, He may plead the whole of His work as God-man and Mediator. Thus He may give us the full benefit of what He has done to sustain the authority of law and to vindicate the character of the Law-giver, as fulfilling conditions that have rendered it possible for God to be just and still justify the penitent sinner.

9. But the plea is directed to the *merciful disposition* of God. He may point to the promise made to him in Isaiah, chap. 52d, from v. 13 to the end, and chap. 53, vs. 1, 2:

" Behold, my servant shall deal prudently, he shall be exalted and extolled, and be very high.

" As many were atonished at thee; (his visage was so marred more than any man, and his form more than the sons of men :)

" So shall he sprinkle many nations; the kings shall shut their mouths at him : for *that* which had not been told them shall they see; and *that* which they had not heard shall they consider.

" Who hath believed our report? and to whom is the arm of the Lord revealed ?

" For he shall grow up before him as a tender plant, and as a root out of a dry ground : he hath no form nor comeliness ; and when we shall see him, *there is* no beauty that we should desire him."

10. He may plead also that He becomes our surety, that He undertakes for us, that He is our wisdom, and righteous-

ness, and sanctification, and redemption; and point to His official relations, His infinite fullness, willingness, and ability to restore us to obedience, and to fit us for the service, the employments, and enjoyments of heaven. It is said that He is made the surety of a better covenant than the legal one; and a covenant founded upon better promises.

11. He may urge as a reason for our pardon the great pleasure it will afford to God, to set aside the execution of the law. "Mercy rejoiceth against judgment." Judgment is His strange work; but He *delighteth* in mercy.

It is said of Victoria that when her prime minister presented a pardon, and asked her if she would sign a pardon in the case of some individual who was sentenced to death, she seized the pen, and said, "Yes! with all my heart!" Could such an appeal be made to a woman's heart, think you, without its leaping for joy to be placed in a position in which it could save the life of a fellow-being?

It is said that "there is joy in the presence of the angels of God over one sinner that repenteth;" and think you not that it affords God the sincerest joy to be able to forgive the wretched sinner, and save him from the doom of hell? He has no pleasure in our death.

It is a grief to Him to be obliged to execute His law on sinners; and no doubt it affords Him infinitely higher pleasure to forgive us, than it does us to be forgiven. He knows full well what are the unutterable horrors of hell and damnation. He knows the sinner can not bear it. He says, "Can thine heart endure, and can thine hands be strong in the day that I shall deal with thee? And what wilt thou do when I shall punish thee?" Our Advocate knows that to punish the sinner is that in which God has no delight—that He will forgive and sign the pardon *with all His heart.*

And think you such an appeal to the heart of God, to His merciful disposition, will have no avail? It is said of Christ, our Advocate, that "for the joy set before Him, He endured the cross, and despised the shame." So great was the love of our Advocate for us that He regarded it a pleasure and a joy so great to save us from hell, that He counted the shame and agony of the cross as a mere trifle—He *despised* them.

This, then, is a disclosure of the *heart* of our Advocate. And how surely may He assume that it will afford God the sincerest joy, *eternal* joy, to be able honorably to seal to us a pardon.

12. He may urge the glory that will redound to the Son of God, for the part that He has taken in this work.

Will it not be eternally honorable in the Son to have advocated the cause of sinners? to have undertaken at so great expense to Himself a cause so desperate? and to have carried it through at the expense of such agony and blood?

Will not the universe of creatures forever wonder and adore, as they see this Advocate surrounded with the *innumerable* throng of souls, for whom His advocacy has prevailed?

13. Our Advocate may plead the gratitude of the redeemed, and the profound thanks and praise of all good beings.

Think you not that the whole family of virtuous beings will forever feel obliged for the intervention of Christ as our Advocate, and for the mercy, forbearance, and love that has saved our race?

CONCLUSION

1. You see what it is to become a Christian. It is to employ Christ as your Advocate, by committing your cause entirely to Him. You can not be saved by your works, you can not be saved by your sufferings, by your prayers—in *any* way except by the intervention of this Advocate. "He ever lives to make intercession for you."

He proposes to undertake your cause; and to be a Christian is to at once surrender your whole cause, your whole life and being to Him as your Advocate.